CHIEF EXECUTIVE TRANSITIONS

How to Hire and Support a Nonprofit CEO

DON TEBBE

BOARDSOURCE®
Building Effective Nonprofit Boards

Library of Congress Cataloging-in-Publication Data

Tebbe, Don.

Chief executive transitions : how to hire and support a nonprofit CEO / Don Tebbe.
    p. cm.

ISBN 1-58686-086-0 (pbk.)

1. Nonprofit organizations—Management. 2. Chief executive officers.
3. Chief executive officers—Recruiting. I. Title.

      HD62.6.T43 2008
      658.4'07—dc22

          2008027056

Published by BoardSource
1828 L Street, NW, Suite 900
Washington, DC 20036

BOARDSOURCE®
Building Effective Nonprofit Boards

BoardSource was established in 1988 by the Association of Governing Boards of Universities and Colleges (AGB) and Independent Sector. Prior to this, in the early 1980s, the two organizations had conducted a survey and found that although 30 percent of respondents believed they were doing a good job of board education and training, the rest of the respondents reported little, if any, activity in strengthening governance. As a result, AGB and IS proposed the creation of a new organization whose mission would be to increase the effectiveness of nonprofit boards.

With a lead grant from the Kellogg Foundation and funding from five other donors, BoardSource opened its doors in 1988 as the National Center for Nonprofit Boards with a staff of three and an operating budget of $385,000. On January 1, 2002, BoardSource took on its new name and identity. These changes were the culmination of an extensive process of understanding how we were perceived, what our audiences wanted, and how we could best meet the needs of nonprofit organizations.

Today BoardSource is the premiere voice of nonprofit governance. Its highly acclaimed products, programs, and services mobilize boards so that organizations fulfill their missions, achieve their goals, increase their impact, and extend their influence. BoardSource is a 501(c)(3) organization.

BoardSource provides

- resources to nonprofit leaders through workshops, training, and an extensive Web site (www.boardsource.org)

- governance consultants who work directly with nonprofit leaders to design specialized solutions to meet an organization's needs

- the world's largest, most comprehensive selection of material on nonprofit governance, including a large selection of books and CD-ROMs

- an annual conference that brings together approximately 900 governance experts, board members, and chief executives and senior staff from around the world

For more information, please visit our Web site at www.boardsource.org, e-mail us at mail@boardsource.org, or call us at 800-883-6262.

Have You Used These BoardSource Resources?

Books

Chief Executive Succession Planning: The Board's Role in Securing Your Organization's Future

The Nonprofit Chief Executive's Ten Basic Responsibilities

Assessment of the Chief Executive

The Board Chair Handbook, Second Edition

Getting the Best from Your Board: An Executive's Guide to a Successful Partnership

Moving Beyond Founder's Syndrome to Nonprofit Success

The Source: Twelve Principles of Governance That Power Exceptional Boards

Exceptional Board Practices: The Source in Action

Fearless Fundraising for Nonprofit Boards, Second Edition

Navigating the Organiational Lifecycle: A Capacity-Building Guide for Nonprofit Leaders

Managing Conflicts of Interest: A Primer for Nonprofit Boards, Second Edition

Driving Strategic Planning: A Nonprofit Executive's Guide

Taming the Troublesome Board Member

The Nonprofit Dashboard: A Tool for Tracking Progress

Meet Smarter: A Guide to Better Nonprofit Board Meetings

The Nonprofit Policy Sampler, Second Edition

The Nonprofit Board Answer Book: A Practical Guide for Board Members and Chief Executives, Second Edition

The Nonprofit Legal Landscape

Self-Assessment for Nonprofit Governing Boards

Understanding Nonprofit Financial Statements, Third Edition

The Nonprofit Board's Guide to Bylaws

Transforming Board Structure: Strategies for Committees and Task Forces

The Board Building Cycle: Nine Steps to Finding, Recruiting, and Engaging Nonprofit Board Members, Second Edition

Culture of Inquiry: Healthy Debate in the Boardroom

The Governance Series

1. *Ten Basic Responsibilities of Nonprofit Boards*
2. *Financial Responsibilities of Nonprofit Boards*
3. *Structures and Practices of Nonprofit Boards*
4. *Fundraising Responsibilities of Nonprofit Boards*
5. *Legal Responsibilities of Nonprofit Boards*
6. *The Nonprofit Board's Role in Setting and Advancing the Mission*
7. *The Nonprofit Board's Role in Planning and Evaluation*
8. *How To Help Your Board Govern More and Manage Less*
9. *Leadership Roles in Nonprofit Governance*

DVDs

Meeting the Challenge: An Orientation to Nonprofit Board Service

Speaking of Money: A Guide to Fundraising for Nonprofit Board Members

For an up-to-date list of publications and information about current prices, membership, and other services, please call BoardSource at 800-883-6262 or visit our Web site at www.boardsource.org.

Contents

Introduction

If your organization is facing a chief executive transition, then welcome to the club. Each year, about 10 percent of nonprofit executive positions change hands — and the rate of turnover is sure to accelerate in the years ahead.

- *The Nonprofit Executive Leadership and Transitions Survey 2004*, a study of 2,200 nonprofit leaders sponsored by the Annie E. Casey Foundation, found that two-thirds of chief executives (65 percent) intended to leave their positions by 2009.

- *Daring to Lead 2006*, published by CompassPoint Nonprofit Services and the Meyer Foundation and based on a survey of 1,900 nonprofit executives, found that 75 percent planned to leave their positions within five years.

- The BoardSource *Nonprofit Governance Index 2007*, a study of over 2,200 board members and chief executives, cited that 49 percent of chief executives see a change in their position in the next five years, while only 30 percent of board members see this change coming.

Clearly, the question is not whether a nonprofit will experience an executive transition, but when. Managing the transition effectively will be crucial to the organization's future impact and continued success. The chief executive, in concert with the board, plays a vital role in defining the organization's strategy, providing the focus for its long-term strategic direction and managing its day-to-day affairs. The handoff from one chief executive to the next is therefore a watershed moment for an organization.

But transitions like these are never easy. According to the *Daring to Lead 2006* survey, 34 percent of nonprofit chief executives leaving their positions are either fired or otherwise forced out. Whether the process is initiated voluntarily or not, successfully managing the departure of a chief executive and the recruitment, hiring, and installation of a replacement is a complicated process that requires months of work. The transition can fail because of a bad fit between the new executive and the organization, or because the board didn't prepare itself to work effectively with its new executive. Such failures can be very costly to the organization.

Among the direct costs of executive transition are advertising, executive search, consulting fees, and relocation expenses. A transition also has "soft costs" such as staff and board time devoted to the transition and hiring process, as well as the time and energy that could otherwise go into fundraising or mission-related activities.

The bottom line: Nonprofit boards need to figure out how to make sure executive transitions are not a problem for their organizations, but rather an opportunity to enhance capacity and add to mission impact down the line.

ABOUT THIS BOOK

This book was created to help board members hire a new chief executive and manage a successful leadership transition. The book is organized in three parts. Part I outlines concepts, ideas, and tools that will help the board make the most of the leadership change. Part II is a hands-on guide to managing the departure of the current executive and initiating a successful transition process. Part III outlines effective approaches to managing the search and hiring process for the new executive. The appendices at the end of the book are designed to assist readers in their search and transition process. For your convenience, all of the appendices are also included on the attached CD-ROM in customizable form.

This book was written with four sets of readers in mind:

1. Board members of nonprofit organizations facing an imminent chief executive transition — either the executive has left or is planning to leave within the next six months. How this book will help: by providing an immediate guide to leading and managing the executive search and transition.

2. Board members facing a chief executive transition that is not imminent — it's either more than six months away or there isn't yet a definitive date. How this book will help: by offering a view of the road ahead, as well as ideas for strengthening your organization and preparing it for a successful transition.

3. Board members who have recently experienced a turnover in chief executives and are looking for ways to help the new executive get off to a better start. How this book will help: by suggesting new approaches to ensuring a longer, more prosperous tenure for your new executive and building a sound partnership between the executive and the board.

4. Board members facing a "non-routine" executive transition — either the executive was terminated or the departure has left the board with serious questions about the organization's circumstances and stability. How this book will help: by offering suggestions about how to drive out the uncertainty and get to a place where the next actions are clear.

Regardless of the particular interest that prompted you to pick up this book, it carries a hopeful message for all readers: While executive transitions pose many risks and challenges, they also are an opportunity to sustain good works and to strengthen organizations so they can increase their mission impact.

Hiring the chief executive may be the most crucial responsibility of a nonprofit board. It is hoped that this book helps your board carry out this responsibility with confidence and great success. Let the journey begin!

Part I.

Planning for Leadership Change

Questions answered in this part of the book:

What is Executive Transition Management (ETM), and how can it help our organization think about managing leadership change in a new way?

How can we use an imminent or looming leadership change as an opportunity to strengthen our organization and get even better results down the road?

What are some of the key principles and guidelines we should be thinking about as we plan our leadership transition?

What special issues should we be thinking about if the departing executive is a founder or long-term leader of the organization?

How can we adapt our plans to the kind of transition we are facing and the unique challenges it presents?

What can we do to make sure we are addressing the need to stabilize the organization and address problematic "legacy issues" we're facing as we embark on this transition?

1.

A New Approach to Managing Leadership Change

As a consultant to organizations facing leadership transitions, I often field phone calls that go something like this: "Hi. This is Sally Smith, board chair of XYZ nonprofit. We had our board meeting last night, and our chief executive announced her resignation."

And then comes the first question: "How quickly can you get an ad in the paper?"

There's a lot going on in this brief message. This is a leader who is clearly anxious and feeling the weight of what may be the most important decision her board will make in its tenure. Most boards experience some level of pain when faced with an executive transition, and their first instinct is to make that pain go away as quickly as possible. But acting hastily can create more problems than it solves — leading to decisions the board could well regret later.

This chapter offers insights on managing leadership change based in part on the principles of Executive Transition Management (ETM). ETM was developed over the past 15 years as a way to help boards better manage chief executive turnover by mitigating the risks and focusing on the opportunities that an executive transition presents.

INTRODUCING EXECUTIVE TRANSITION MANAGEMENT

An executive transition involves a series of events that begins with the incumbent executive's decision to depart (or the board's decision to force a change) and concludes after the succeeding executive has settled into the new job. The timeframe for the entire transition process can be a matter of months, or several years in the case of a retiring executive who is planning a departure but who won't be leaving for a while (see Appendix 1 for a sample transition timeline).

Executive transitions are naturally occurring events that have to do with human nature, organizational circumstance and a variety other factors. The goals of Executive Transition Management are (1) to help boards recognize these events as crucial turning points for their organizations, and (2) to provide the tools boards need to manage the process so it produces good outcomes for the organization.

ETM is more than an executive search; it's a way of managing the entire turnover and handoff process in a manner that builds the capacity of the organization. The ETM process is based on a three-phase model for managing the entire departure, search, selection, hiring, and on-boarding process. ETM takes the board from early-stage thinking about executive succession through the successful launch of the incoming executive.

The chart below illustrates the phases and sequence of Executive Transition Management, as well as the goal to build organizational capacity.

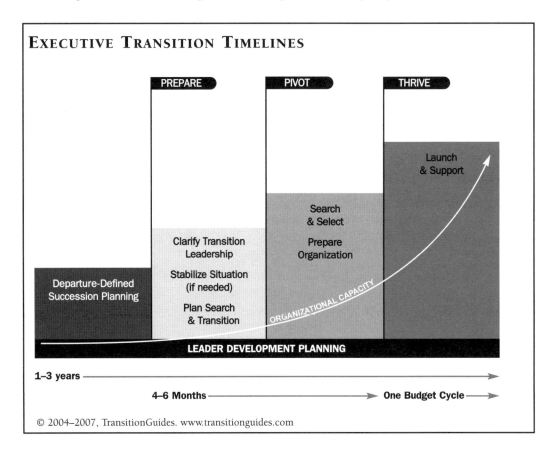

EXECUTIVE TRANSITION TIMELINES

| PREPARE | PIVOT | THRIVE |

Launch & Support

Search & Select

Prepare Organization

Clarify Transition Leadership

Stabilize Situation (if needed)

Plan Search & Transition

Departure-Defined Succession Planning

ORGANIZATIONAL CAPACITY

LEADER DEVELOPMENT PLANNING

1–3 years

4–6 Months

One Budget Cycle

© 2004–2007, TransitionGuides. www.transitionguides.com

The three phases of Executive Transition Management are as follows:

- *Prepare* — In this phase, the board works to ensure that the organization is ready to hire a new executive and is prepared to start the search. Ideally, the organization has explored succession planning well ahead of the departure (a year or more), particularly if the departure involves a founder or long-term executive.

- *Pivot* — This phase has two goals (1) conduct a robust search and hiring process that results in the selection of a new executive, and (2) prepare the organization to work more effectively with the new leader by addressing "legacy issues" (see box, page 5) that might impact the executive's performance.

- *Thrive* — In this phase, the board designs and implements an effective orientation and launch for the new executive. The goal here is to ensure that the board and executive get off to the right start by clarifying priorities, as well as their respective roles and responsibilities, and their expectations and plans for monitoring and evaluating performance.

Remember the phone call from Sally? The anxiety she feels about the departure of her organization's executive stems from her recognition of the potential risks involved in the transition. Her sense of urgency is a natural human response to change. Her immediate focus on the need for a search is a natural outgrowth of the anxiety and urgency she feels.

The ETM model, however, is designed to enable Sally and other board members like her to pull back and see the bigger picture. The transition becomes a project Sally can manage like any other project, working with her colleagues on the board to think about their choices and how to proceed — and about the opportunities, not just the risks, that the transition presents for the organization.

"LEGACY ISSUES" DEFINED

Legacy issues are leftover issues from the previous executive's tenure that, if left unattended, might hinder the new executive's performance. Legacy issues can include small systemic problems such as limited tracking and reporting of financial information, a problem that can be easily resolved via updated accounting software or a redesign of existing management reports. Larger legacy issues can include a board whose membership does not fit with the expanded fund-development role it needs to play for the organization. Some of these large-scale changes may require outside consultation or expertise to resolve. (See page 35 for a discussion of working with consultants.)

KEY PRINCIPLES OF ETM

The following are some of the principles that underpin the ETM process and that board members should keep in mind as they approach a transition:

Leading a transition requires a larger view. Faced with an executive transition, the board's natural tendency is to focus immediately on advertising the position. But a successful executive transition requires more than just a successful search. In reality, an executive transition is a series of decisions and actions that begin with the executive's decision to depart (or the board's decision to terminate) and conclude with the completion of the first full budget or business cycle under the new executive's leadership. Executive search is one element of that process — a major centerpiece but still only one element. Focusing on the whole of the transition — planning and preparation, executive search, and executive installation and support — provides for better outcomes.

Transitions involve not just risks, but rewards, too. The departure of an executive can be challenging, but it is also a time of great opportunity. Executive Transition Management is about managing the risks and capturing the rewards presented by the departure of one executive and the subsequent hiring of a successor.

What are the risks of a failed transition? They include a bad fit between the executive and the job; a loss of stakeholder support; a loss of funding; brain drain resulting from the departure of disaffected key staff; a downward spiral in efficiency leading to reduced mission impact; loss of momentum; and, in the worst-case scenario, failure of the entire organization.

Balanced against these risks are the potential opportunities presented by a successful transition. If properly managed and proactively led, an executive transition can become an important and useful moment for an organization. It is an opportunity to pause and perhaps regroup. With expert support as needed, board members can assess the organization from a new perspective. They can work through the hiring process in a way that enables the organization to implement new strategies, or go in new directions that enable the organization not only to endure the transition but also to emerge stronger.

Transitions have a profound human dimension — it's not all about process. Board members should keep in mind that transitions always provoke emotions. There can be a sense of loss tied to the departure of a beloved executive, there can be frustration because an executive's tenure is ending badly, and there can be hope and optimism among the board and staff about the organization's future under new leadership.

RULES OF THUMB FOR SUCCESSFUL TRANSITIONS

Successful executive transitions don't happen by accident. As the ETM model shows, they require solid planning and lots of good thinking about where the organization is, where it wants to go, and what kind of leadership it needs to get there.

Here are some guidelines that can help board members navigate the transition process toward a successful conclusion:

Don't rush the process. Usually there's great pressure to move quickly to place ads and begin recruiting. If a board is concerned about a potential gap in executive leadership, it should consider hiring an interim executive to take the pressure off and give the board the time to be deliberate. (See Chapter 5 for more on interim executives.) Rushing the process can lead to sloppy decision making and can cause the board to settle for a lesser candidate in its rush to fill the position. Tom Gilmore, author of *Making a Leadership Change: How Organizations and Leaders Can Handle Leadership Transitions Successfully*, describes the rash decision making that can occur during the transition as "sleepwalking through the process."

Strive for a good ending, so that you can have a good beginning. How an organization ends the relationship with its current executive will say a lot about the board — to that executive, to the staff, and to the community. Obviously, the departing executive bears some responsibility for how the departure goes, but the board has the primary duty for setting the tone. This means striving for the most positive ending possible even in the messiest departures, because the organization's ending with one executive will impact the beginning with the next. Taking the high road with an executive who has behaved badly sets a positive, intentional tone for the future and communicates to the organization's stakeholders that this is a board that has its values in the right place. On the other hand, if the departing executive is a beloved, longtime leader, the board needs to make sure that person is appropriately acknowledged through ceremonies, events, and other activities that allow people to come to closure.

Engage the staff and reap rewards. While the board shoulders the principal responsibility for leading the chief executive transition, no other group has more at stake in the outcome of this process than the staff. Boards should treat the staff as an important asset during the transition. Staff members are a rich source of information about the organization and its day-to-day operations. Finding an appropriate way to engage staff in the transition can help ensure that the board's decisions reflect the organization's actual needs. Moreover, the act of engaging staff can help reduce staff members' anxiety and build their buy-in for the transition outcome. During transition planning, boards should consider including one or more staff members on the transition committee. Staff members also should be involved in preparing the organization before the new executive arrives (for example, by working with the board to address legacy issues) and in the orientation process for the incoming executive.

Begin with the end in mind. The desired outcome of an executive transition should not just be finding a replacement for the departing executive. Hiring a successor is the most obvious result of the transition, but the ETM approach is founded on the idea that the process should put the organization on a stronger footing as well. Therefore, boards should enter the transition process with some of the following goals in mind:

- Finding and hiring a new executive who fits the current and future leadership needs of the organization

- Addressing organizational issues that come to light during the transition, and putting any problems on track toward resolution

- Securing the commitment of the board and staff to work effectively with the new executive

- Achieving agreement between the board and the new executive about priorities, roles, expectations, and performance measures

Come to terms with history. The departure of one executive and the arrival of the next mark the end of one chapter in an organization's history and the opening of a new one. Harking back to the past too much can make the new chapter more of a slog for all involved. This means boards should watch out for inappropriate comparisons of the new executive against the merits of the old. While honoring what's been accomplished and applying lessons from the past, the board should use the transition to close the books on the departing executive's tenure and give the new executive a fresh set of pages to work with. In the event of a messy departure, it's important to deal in a forward-looking way with the issues that may have precipitated it, rather than re-fighting old battles.

A successful search ≠ a successful transition. One approach to executive transitions is for the board to focus on the search and leave everything else in the hands of the new chief executive. Call it "savior thinking" — if only we get the right person, all of our problems will be solved. But a board can conclude a successful search and still face the risk of a failed transition if it hasn't paid attention to the environment that the new leader is stepping into. The organization, for example, may need to come to grips with persistent issues or past behaviors that will inhibit the effectiveness of the new executive. Another possibility is that the board may be asking the new executive to take on an impossible task. In this case, the board may want to consider redefining the job or creating a deputy executive slot.

Step up and support the new executive. After the search is complete, boards often are tempted to breathe a sigh of relief and get back to business as usual. However, with a new executive in place, there is no business as usual. The first few months are the most critical of the new executive's tenure. It is a time when the die is cast on important relationships, especially those between the board and the executive and between the executive and staff. During this time, the board and the executive should set out to create a good working relationship — clarifying goals, roles, expectations, and performance measures. (See Chapter 7 for more on launching and keeping the new executive.) New executives may need additional support to settle in, professional development to round out their skill sets, and/or coaching or mentoring to address specific challenges. The board should initiate the relationship-building work and let the executive know it's open to providing the needed support.

WHEN THE DEPARTING EXECUTIVE IS A FOUNDER OR LONG-TERM LEADER

Special considerations apply in transitions involving a founder or an executive who has been in the position for more than five to seven years. Research and anecdotal evidence suggest that founder-led organizations often have weaker boards that are highly reliant on the founder's vision, direction, and leadership. Moreover, in these organizations, the programs, systems, and other aspects of the organization are sometimes a reflection of the interests, perhaps even the idiosyncrasies, of the founder.

Founder-led organizations also often have boards that are populated with friends of the founder. In these cases, the transition may be a time for the board itself to change so that it can become an independent-thinking board that has its own sense of itself and its relationship to the organization. The board may also benefit from board development training. One important focus for training and discussion: sorting out the board's role in relation to the role of the executive and building an effective board-executive partnership.

Similarly, transitions involving long-term chief executives can present their own special challenges. Chief executives are responsibility magnets. Over the years, responsibilities get attached to them that may not necessarily fit the role of the incoming executive. In these cases, it's important for the board to work with the departing executive and the staff to "unpack" the job. Transitions often call on the board to find homes for a variety of responsibilities that departing executives have collected unto themselves over the years.

CONCLUSION

The ETM model yields important insights about what makes for a successful executive transition. Perhaps the most important insight of all is that successful transitions have distinct phases, with each one building on the one before. The search for a new executive, while central to the process, does not in itself determine a successful transition. Rather, the process begins with the board working to stabilize the organization and plan for a smooth transition. And it doesn't end until the board has ensured that the new executive has everything he or she needs to get off to a strong start. Cutting corners at any point in the process can put the success of the transition at risk. On the other hand, to the extent that the board devotes sufficient time and energy to every part of the process — from transition planning through the orientation and launch of the new executive — the transition can become a springboard enabling the organization to reach new heights.

2.

Getting Started: Planning the Transition

After the board has been informed of the resignation of the chief executive or after it makes the decision to initiate a leadership change, it is time to take stock of the situation. The board will start by identifying what kind of transition the organization is facing, as well as what issues it needs to address in order to ensure that the new executive can start the job on firm footing. This assessment will help board members determine the actions they need to take to stabilize the organization (if necessary) and to fill the interim executive leadership role (if required).

This chapter provides an overview of some of the key considerations for the board as it launches the transition planning process.

KNOW YOUR TRANSITION TYPE

The type of transition that an organization is facing influences the costs of the transition, as well as the challenges involved and the ultimate strategy the board will adopt to manage the process. Below are five classic transition types and their associated key challenges.

PRIORITIES FOR TRANSITION PLANNING

In addition to fine-tuning its understanding of the nature of the transition, the board should use the early transition planning period to address the following priorities:

Stabilize the organization. A critical aspect of any organization's readiness to hire is whether or not the organization is stable. Questions for the board include the following: What's going on with the organization? Are there immediate concerns about the organization's viability? Is it facing a financial crisis? Is it politically under fire? Is it facing some other threat? What's the emotional climate on the staff and board? Is there turmoil over the circumstances of the executive's departure?

An organization's leadership team may be too distracted by doubts about its stability to embark on a successful transition. If board and staff are engaged in infighting, or if they are still reacting to past events, they can't be expected to approach the planning process with the appropriate frame of mind. In these situations, the board needs to attend to the organization's stability needs first.

Achieving stability may take time. If the incumbent executive has already departed or will soon do so, the board should consider hiring a skilled interim director to provide some breathing room and help settle things down. (See Chapter 5 for more on the role of interim executives.)

FIVE CLASSIC TRANSITION TYPES

THE TYPE	THE SITUATION
TYPE 1: "SUSTAINED SUCCESS"	• Organization is well led. • Most or all components are performing well or at an exemplary level. • Transition discussions are peppered with comments such as, "We can't afford to miss a beat."
TYPE 2: "UNDERPERFORMING ORGANIZATION"	• Organization may be performing poorly or it may have peaked and could start to decline without a change in strategy. • Funders, board members, and key staff may be wondering if the organization is doing enough, and if its work and strategies have "gone stale" and need to be revitalized. • Transition discussions usually include worried statements about the organization's business model or operating methods.
TYPE 3: "TURNAROUND"	• Organizational performance has reached a perilous state. • External conditions may have deteriorated, causing a decline in support or a surge in demand for services that the organization cannot meet. • Alternatively, mismanagement or a scandal involving the organization may have caused a crisis in confidence and morale.

THE KEY CHALLENGES FOR THE BOARD

1. Resist the temptation to try to find someone just like the departing executive. The skills, abilities, and attributes that got the organization where it is today may not be what it needs to move forward. The question at the heart of the transition is not how to fill the departing executive's shoes. Rather, the board should be asking where the organization is headed and what kind of leadership it needs to get there.

2. Take a hard look at the executive's responsibilities and workload. In a "sustained success" situation, the board should make every effort to make sure the executive job is doable — for example, by eliminating extraneous duties that may have accumulated for a long-tenured executive, or by augmenting the senior leadership team to provide the new executive with operational support.

---

1. Diagnose the problems. The main challenge in this situation is to properly diagnose the underlying issues facing the organization and to make sure they are addressed during the transition.

2. Reorient the executive's job to fit the organization's needs. Underlying questions about the organization's work and approach should be considered in the design of the incoming chief executive's job and the preparation of the organization to work more effectively with a new executive. These questions also should be discussed openly with the candidates during the hiring process and factored into post-hire planning.

---

1. Stabilize the organization. Whatever the challenges or the precise situation facing the organization, it must be stable before deep transition planning can begin. The board needs to acknowledge the crisis, understand the underlying factors, and meet them head-on. If there are funding challenges, the board may need to make special appeals to funders. Sometimes, the challenges are so severe that the best course is to merge with or be acquired by a stronger organization that can provide new resources, a sound infrastructure, and broader reach.

2. Establish interim leadership. The organization needs appropriate leadership during the transition. Turnarounds are not a situation for a novice manager. The board should therefore consider bringing in a skilled interim executive or consultant to help.

3. Improve staff morale. Staff can be demoralized in a turnaround situation, feeling let down by a departing executive or the board, or both. One priority for the board: reducing "brain drain" by limiting turnover of key personnel.

4. Avoid the "pendulum swing." Often, a board facing a turnaround brought on by problems with a departing executive will try to find that person's mirror opposite to lead the organization into the future — for example, by hiring for financial skills while overlooking other important leadership attributes. The better approach is to focus on the full set of skills required to get the organization to where the board believes it needs to be.

5. Be honest. Honesty is the best policy as the board confronts the challenges facing the organization. People will respect and are willing to help an organization in a turnaround when they see diligent action, honest communications, and a positive attitude.

THE TYPE	THE SITUATION
TYPE 4 **"FIRST HIRE"**	• Organization is a start-up or is shifting from all-volunteer management to a hired executive.
TYPE 5 **"HARD-TO-FOLLOW** **EXECUTIVE"**	• Organization is facing the departure of a founder, a highly entrepreneurial executive, or a long-tenured leader (seven or more years in the role) • The looming departure presages major change as the organization's culture, performance expectations, relationships, and perhaps even its structure are a reflection of the departing leader's thinking and personality.

The Key Challenges for the Board

1. Clarify the executive job. Hiring a chief executive for a start-up or all-volunteer organization presents its own unique challenges for the board. The first is defining the job. The chief executive may be the only paid position or one of a very few. It is essential to make the job doable and one that can actually be filled.

2. Look for experience. "First hire" executives can face intense demands. With no management structure currently in place, and with the organization's programs and strategies not yet clearly defined (in the case of start-up organizations), the questions facing the new leader can be overwhelming. Because this can be such a risky and demanding time, the board should consider candidates with start-up experience. An alternative is to contract with a seasoned executive to help get the organization off the ground before the permanent hire is made.

3. Manage expectations. For all-volunteer organizations, it's important to make sure the board and the volunteer base understand that having a hired executive cannot lead to improved performance and greater impact overnight. The founders and volunteers of the organization also may have a hard time letting go as the new executive takes over; there needs to be acceptance that roles will shift and the culture may change. Bottom line: The board should craft the job description very carefully and ensure that everyone understands the new executive's role.

---

1. Ensure the organization is stable. Faced with the departure of a hard-to-follow leader, even the most stable organization can become vulnerable. The board should assess the situation carefully, identify vulnerabilities created by the departure (e.g., lost relationships with key partners or donors), and work to address them.

2. Sort out and reassign responsibilities as needed. A second challenge is to understand the departing executive's role and impact in the organization and to find a new home for some of that person's accumulated responsibilities, as described in Chapter 1.

3. Think anew about board and executive roles. The biggest challenge for the board in these situations may be to break out of its business-as-usual mentality, and to understand the need to thoroughly rethink its governance role and the board-executive relationship with a new executive in place.

Stability questions are not limited to organizations in crisis, however. All organizations need to consider the executive's workload, as well as deadlines and other obligations that might come due during the transition. Moreover, during times of transition, weaknesses in other parts of the organization often become readily apparent. For example, a particularly strong chief executive might be propping up a weak management team, or the organization may have inefficient systems it's been making do with for far too long.

Identify legacy issues and map corrective actions. Finding a talented executive who is ready to assume the leadership role is an absolutely essential ingredient of a successful executive transition. Preparing the organization to work effectively with the new leader can be just as crucial. As described in Chapter 1, boards embarking on a transition should set out to identify legacy issues, which, if left unattended, might hinder the new executive's performance. Some of these issues can and should be addressed before the new executive is hired. Other issues may be too big to tackle during this interim period, but boards will need to keep them front and center while figuring out the kind of leadership that will best serve the organization going forward, as well as priorities for the new executive. (For a definition and examples of legacy issues, see page 5.)

Map the chief executive's job. Even the most actively engaged boards can be uncertain about the scope of the chief executive's role. Facing a transition, the board doesn't have to understand the job at its most granular level, but board members do need to develop a good sense of the leadership demands that the next executive is going to face.

Rick Moyers, in *The Nonprofit Chief Executive's Ten Basic Responsibilities* (BoardSource, 2006), outlines the executive's responsibilities as

1. Commit to the mission.

2. Lead the staff and manage the organization.

3. Exercise responsible financial stewardship.

4. Lead and manage fundraising.

5. Follow the highest ethical standards, ensure accountability, and comply with the law.

6. Engage the board in planning and lead the implementation.

7. Develop future leadership.

8. Build external relationships and serve as an advocate.

9. Ensure the quality and effectiveness of programs.

10. Support the board.

A number of factors frame the role of the chief executive; some of these can be found in the job description, but many cannot. Job descriptions typically cover authority, responsibilities, and reporting relationships. Other factors typically not covered in the job description have to do with the leadership challenge facing the organization — i.e., what the board wants the new executive to accomplish. As a result, the board should take some time at the start of the transition process to think hard about the precise responsibilities that the new executive's job will entail.

Connect transition planning to overall strategy. If the board was recently (and deeply) engaged in strategic or long-range planning, then the board's transition planning work might start with revisiting key elements of the strategic plan and moving directly into a discussion about the implications for the next executive's leadership role. If a strategic plan is nonexistent or out of date, the transition planning work will need to begin at a more fundamental level.

Board and staff leaders can clarify current and future leadership needs by focusing on the following three sets of strategic questions in a series of meetings or a mini-retreat:

1. Where do we stand as an organization? What's our mission? Who are our customers? What are our successes? What are our core competencies? What are our strengths and weaknesses?

2. Where are we headed? What's our long-term strategic direction? What is our vision for the next three to five years? What challenges are we facing on the immediate horizon? What are the opportunities to capture? What does future success look like?

3. What kind of leadership do we need? If there is a gap between our present and our desired future, what kind of leadership will it take to close the gap? What does our assessment of where we stand and where we are headed tell us about any pivots or changes the board may need to make? What does it tell us about the priorities for the first year of the new executive's tenure?

Prepare the board. Ensuring that the board is prepared to launch a powerful relationship with its incoming executive can have a profound influence on that person's success. The transition plan should therefore include specific actions aimed at preparing the board, such as

- providing training about board responsibilities versus executive responsibilities for a board that has traditionally micromanaged

- forming a development committee and a plan for ramping up the organization's fundraising program through more active board involvement

- scaling back a board that identified itself as too large and disinterested

- recruiting and training new board members for a board that had suffered serious attrition

DOCUMENTING THE OUTCOMES OF TRANSITION PLANNING

Boards should consider documenting the results of their early transition planning discussions in the following way:

- A narrative statement (three to five paragraphs) that lays out the leadership opportunity (or challenge) for the next executive

- A list of key characteristics, skills, and other attributes that the board is seeking in the candidates

- An initial list of priority items that the board would like to see accomplished early in the new executive's tenure

- A list of the board's insights about how its own role might evolve (Some of these observations might become legacy issues to be addressed in the interim period before the new executive starts.)

CONCLUSION

Selecting and launching a new executive is among the most risky activities that a board can face. The risks of a bad hire can be greatly reduced when the board clearly understands its current and future leadership needs and calibrates the transition process accordingly. A board that has endeavored to complete the activities outlined in this chapter should be well on its way to addressing key issues that can determine the success or failure of the transition. These activities do not have to take a lot of time, and yet the results they yield are enormous. The rich understanding resulting from early assessment and planning work will empower the board to make a better choice and will set the stage for a thriving relationship with the new executive.

~ Part I Checklist ~
Planning for Leadership Change

At this point in the process, the board has

✓ identified the type of transition the organization is facing, along with the challenges and the opportunities involved

✓ initiated efforts to stabilize the organization, if needed

✓ developed a strong sense of the responsibilities that had accrued to the departing executive and initiated efforts to shift responsibilities to other staff, as needed, to make the job more doable

✓ conducted an organizational review or assessment that outlines the organization's situation, strengths and assets, and opportunities, while flagging legacy issues that, if addressed, would help make the new executive more successful

✓ reached agreement about the organization's strategic direction, desired attributes for the new executive, key priorities for the executive's first 12 to 18 months, and potential changes the board itself might need to make

Part II.

Managing the Departure and Transition

Questions answered in this part of the book:

What should we be doing in the first few days after the executive's departure is official to make sure the transition gets off to a positive start?

What are the best ways to make the departure known to the organization's key audiences, including donors, staff, the media, and others?

What is the role of the board in leading the transition process? And what should we be thinking about as we appoint a transition committee to manage the process?

To what extent should the departing executive be involved in the transition — and in what ways?

Should we appoint a temporary chief executive to lead the organization during the transition?

What should we look for in a temporary executive, and where can we find a person with the right qualifications?

3.

Departure Management and Communications

Every transition begins with a departure. Maybe it's a planned departure where the executive has given ample notice. On the other hand, it could be an abrupt departure, with the executive leaving quickly to pursue a new opportunity. Or the departure may involve challenging circumstances such as the firing of the executive because of poor performance, improprieties, or perhaps even a scandal. In some extremely unfortunate circumstances, the transition may have been precipitated by the death or serious illness of the executive.

This chapter describes early-stage departure management and planning, activities that typically would be completed in the first five days of the transition. The chapter also includes a discussion of communications issues relating to the departure and transition.

ANNOUNCING THE DEPARTURE

Good communication is an important ingredient of a successful transition. An organization's key stakeholders — including major donors, key institutional funders and any collaboration partners — will want to hear about the transition early and from the board directly. Allowing these stakeholders to find out about the departure through the grapevine might seriously affect the organization's important relationships.

DISCOVERING WHAT YOU DON'T KNOW

To some degree, every board facing an executive transition has to come to grips with what it knows and doesn't know about the organization. Even the most highly engaged and effective board may need to develop a deeper understanding of the organization and the executive job in order to manage the transition. In departures involving an executive termination, a turnaround, or an underperforming organization, there may be surprises in store for the board as it begins to assess the organization. The board may discover that the organization is not as financially stable as it had been led to believe, or that its understanding of the strength of the staff team or operations was off the mark. Especially in the case of the organization's finances, the board will need to satisfy its questions and drive out any uncertainty before effective planning can take place. Planning on top of critical uncertainties is a recipe for disaster.

MANAGING THE DEPARTURE: THE FIRST FIVE DAYS

The first five days after an executive's departure becomes official are a crucial time. Regardless of the circumstances, the departure management process is the same: organize, stabilize, understand, plan, and execute.

THE ABRUPT DEPARTURE

If an executive has left or is leaving abruptly, the first step for the board should always be to pull out its emergency succession or backup plan for the executive role, if one exists, and begin to follow it. The key to success in these challenging circumstances is for the board to pay attention to the principle described in Chapter 1: *Strive for a good ending so you can have a good beginning.* This means trying for the best possible ending with the departing executive so there is a sense of completion with no unfinished business. Key steps include

Organize

- Appoint a transition committee (traditionally known as the search committee).

- Hold organizing meeting(s) to address the following steps.

- Resolve any key problems with the exiting leader before transition planning can begin in earnest.

- Address the need for interim leadership by hiring an interim chief executive or appointing an acting chief executive.

Stabilize

- Address any financial crises facing the organization.

- Attend to the staff by arranging a meeting where the board chair and/or other board leaders can hear the staff's story and concerns, provide appropriate assurance, and inform staff of initial plans for the transition.

- Meet with/contact key funders to make sure they are informed and aware that the board is taking decisive action.

Understand

- Make sure the board understands the organization's financial situation, its contracts, and other external obligations.

- Review personnel policies to ensure that the board understands the organization's obligations to the departing executive for unpaid leave, insurance, etc.

- If possible, conduct an exit interview with the departing executive to acquire critical information, such as the status of contracts.

- Secure legal advice to discuss the terms of separation and to review related documents if the board is discharging the executive.

- Inform the auditor of the situation and determine if a special audit may be needed.

Plan

- Develop an initial timeline covering at least the first phase of the transition, including assignments for board and staff. (This can be a living document that the board updates as the situation becomes clearer and uncertainties have been addressed.)

- Prepare a public statement and talking points about the departure to ensure that all board members are on the same page in their communications.

- Identify a spokesperson to respond to media inquiries, if necessary (see below for more on communications).

Execute

- Work the plan.

- Communicate with the staff and key stakeholders.

- Provide assurance that the board is working diligently to make sure the organization will come out of this situation in good shape, and even stronger.

- Update any funders with whom the organization has grants or contracts.

- Secure keys and computer passwords from the departing executive, as well as any organizational property such as credit cards, laptop, cell phone, etc.

- Change the signatories on all financial accounts.

THE PLANNED DEPARTURE

In the event of a departure where the executive is giving several months' notice, the board has more time to launch and execute its transition plan. But the initial planning and assessment process is just as urgent.

Organize

- Appoint a transition committee.

- Hold organizing meeting(s) to address the following steps.

- Define the departing executive's role during the transition.

Stabilize

- Attend to the staff.

- Consider having the board chair and/or other board leaders meet with the staff along with departing chief executive, if necessary.

- Review plans for addressing any current staff vacancies.

Understand

- Assess the organization — its finances, systems, staffing, governance, and current strategic direction.

- Unpack the current chief executive's job and encourage delegation of extraneous duties.

- Ask the departing executive to develop a handoff report that outlines key contacts, grants and contracts, major deadlines, internal and external liabilities and obligations, and the executive's sense of the organization's current situation and future direction.

Plan

- Develop an initial timeline covering at least the first phase of the transition, including assignments for board and staff. (This can be a living document that the board updates as the situation becomes clearer and uncertainties have been addressed.)

- Prepare a public statement and talking points about the departure to ensure that all board members are on the same page in their communications.

- Identify a spokesperson, typically the departing executive and/or board chair, to respond to media inquiries, if necessary (see below for more on communications).

Execute

- Work the plan.

- Communicate with the staff and key stakeholders.

- Provide assurance that the board is working diligently to plan a successful transition.

- Work with the departing executive to inform any funders with whom the organization has grants or contracts.

At the same time, the board should do some careful, albeit quick, planning before announcing the transition. The goal is to communicate with clarity and in a way that inspires confidence among stakeholders. The board does not need a detailed transition plan at this point, just a list of top-level actions that will help stakeholders see how the organization plans to handle the transition, along with a rough timetable. If appropriate, the board also can inform stakeholders about how they can be helpful to the organization during the transition.

Except in cases of involuntary separation between the organization and the departing executive, the executive is normally the one who drives the departure communications. The executive and the board chair should work together on a rough outline or understanding about how the departure communications will be handled. Usually the process starts with phone calls to board members, followed by an announcement to the staff. This is followed by calls to individual key stakeholders, such as major donors. In these calls, the board chair and/or departing executive might request a face-to-face meeting to update donors on transition preparations, planning, and timing.

In challenging circumstances involving the involuntary departure of an executive or a scandal or organizational crisis, communications with staff, key funders, and others takes on heightened importance. A natural tendency for the board would be to deal with the messy ending first and get things settled, then communicate. Meanwhile, however, the rumor mill may be gearing up, funders may be hearing things, and the word on the street may be that the organization is in trouble. A better approach is to communicate appropriately while the board is dealing with the circumstances. The board does not need to air the organization's dirty laundry. Rather, the priority should be to give key constituencies what they're looking for: assurance that the board is on top of the situation and engaged in thoughtful planning.

DEVELOPING A COMMUNICATIONS PLAN AND MATERIALS

To communicate about the departure and transition, the organization needs a plan, plus the necessary support materials, as described below. An organization can gain a good head start on the communications process by having key lists and documents prepared ahead of time, even before a transition.

1. **The communications plan:** The plan can be as simple as a half-page outline of key communications actions, the audiences the organization needs to reach, who is responsible for which actions, and due dates for each. The plan should also clearly outline who is responsible to speak on behalf of the organization. This needs to be communicated to the staff, particularly those answering the phones, so calls can be routed to the right person.

2. **The support materials:** Support materials for departure communications usually consist of

   a. A letter addressed to key stakeholders. This might actually be several letters, one sent by the departing executive to one set of close-in stakeholders and a second, more general letter signed by the board chair and sent to a wider list.

b. A one-page set of talking points. This helps ensure that everyone involved in the communications process is clear about the key points and stays on message. The talking points usually include a statement or statements acknowledging the departing executive's contributions to the organization. The statement also should describe the board's plans for managing the transition. Where possible, the talking points should include something about what's next for the departing executive. (Talking points are particularly important in controversial departures — i.e., if the board wants to say that the chief executive is retiring and the chief executive doesn't see it that way.)

c. A press release. The organization should draft a press release covering many of the talking points noted above and send it to key news outlets.

3. **The list:** An organization's list of contacts for communications about the departure and transition could potentially be huge, with many names, groups, and categories included. To get a better handle on the list and prioritize key contacts, the board should consider grouping stakeholders according to the actions it will take to communicate the departure.

a. The phone list. Typically, this is a short list of the organization's most important stakeholders — those who should be called personally and informed of the departure. The departing chief executive may make these calls if departing in good circumstances. If the chief executive has already left, or if there was a messy ending, then the calls should probably be made by the board chair, transition committee chair, or another board member who may have a close relationship with the individual stakeholder in question.

b. The letter list. This list of stakeholders will receive a letter from the departing executive, board chair, or other board member, as appropriate.

c. The newsletter list. This list usually includes categories of individuals rather than actual names — e.g., community members, clients. This group will be informed through the organization's newsletter or other means.

d. The media list. This is a list of media outlets that will receive the press release and/or phone calls from the organization's spokesperson or spokespersons, as appropriate.

ANNOUNCING THE DEPARTURE TO STAFF

One of an organization's most important set of stakeholders is the staff. Of any group, the staff probably have the most at stake in the transition — professionally and personally — and probably feel the most vulnerable. The departure of the chief executive, whether beloved or controversial, can leave the organization feeling a bit unglued. The board will want to ensure stability and calm among the staff.

For this reason, it is vitally important to have a board member, ideally the board chair, on hand to announce the departure to the staff and answer questions. The announcement also could be made by the departing chief executive (if leaving on good terms). The board chair would then speak to the organization's plans for the transition, the role staff might play during the transition process, and other issues.

If the departure involves some controversy, or if the chief executive has been terminated, several board members might be involved in the departure announcement and then have follow-up, one-on-one meetings with management team members and other key staff. Abrupt departures are unsettling and potentially destabilizing to the staff. It typically takes more than one session with the staff to help settle things down.

The board should keep two concepts in mind as it weighs how best to communicate with the staff: empathy and assurance. Empathy means allowing the staff to voice their concerns about the transition, to ask questions, and to have the opportunity to dialog with the board leadership about the transition. Assurance means providing staff members with a solid game plan for the transition and clarity about what's expected of them during the weeks and months ahead. If there is any question about the organization's stability, the board should communicate how it is addressing key problems and vulnerabilities and its timetable for resolving them.

CONCLUSION

The board's responsibilities in the first few days after knowing that an executive will be leaving are clear. The framework of organize, stabilize, understand, plan, and execute provides a road map to successful management for abrupt and planned departures alike. In addition, the board should take seriously its responsibility to communicate with key stakeholders in a way that inspires confidence in the organization's capacity to manage the transition to a successful conclusion. Funders and staff deserve special attention as the board sets out to convey reassuring messages about the organization's plans and future.

4.

Transition Leadership: Who's in Charge?

Executive transitions call on the board to step up to a higher level of engagement and to lead the organization through a crucial period that will determine its future course. While much of the board's work will be carried out through the work of the transition committee, the larger board still has an important role to play throughout the process. At the same time, there is also an important role in the transition for the departing chief executive, if that person is leaving the organizing on friendly terms.

This chapter explores the roles and responsibilities of the board, the transition committee and the departing executive in the leadership of the transition. Chapter 5 describes the role of a temporary executive.

TRANSITION LEADERSHIP: THE BOARD

Leading the transition involves more than just appointing a transition committee and then voting on its recommendation when the search is complete. Rather, the board's role is to set out the expectations that define success for the transition, and to ensure that the process addresses any legacy issues facing the organization.

As described in Chapter 2, the board should ensure that transition planning takes into consideration where the organization stands and where it is headed, and that the job of the incoming executive is calibrated to address the organization's future direction. The board also should ensure that diversity and cultural competency considerations are factored into the planning work, chiefly by insisting on a diverse pool of finalists. Finally, the board has an important role to play in making sure that the organization is stable during the transition (especially in situations of an abrupt transition or a messy departure) and in communicating with key audiences, as described in Chapter 3.

At the same time that the board is stepping into its leadership role in the transition, it also must engage in a thorough assessment of its own practices and the extent to which it is prepared to work with a new executive. Research by BoardSource, published in the *Nonprofit Governance Index 2007*, has found that chief executives spend nearly one-quarter of their time on board-related work. Clearly, the board is not only an incredibly important part of the leadership team, it is also a major influence in the chief executive's work life.

Preparing the board to work with a new chief executive shouldn't be viewed as a remediation effort. Rather, it should be undertaken with an eye toward building a positive, forward-looking relationship with the incoming executive.

Among the questions that should guide the board's discussions are the following: What is the board's strategic contribution toward the vision of the organization? How should the board govern in light of that vision and the type of executive it is trying to recruit? The answers to these larger questions will go a long way to shaping constructive preparation work and providing the energy and excitement the board needs to push forward with any changes in its structure, practices, or approach.

TRANSITION LEADERSHIP: THE TRANSITION COMMITTEE

Once the board has a better understanding of the nature of the transition and some of the organization's priorities moving forward, it needs to assemble a transition committee that will plan and oversee the process. *This book purposely uses the term "transition committee" as opposed to "search committee" to convey clearly that the committee's attention should be on the entire transition process, not just the few months of executive search.*

The transition committee is an ad hoc committee whose purpose is to plan and oversee the entire executive transition process. Typically, the duration of the committee's appointment is from the beginning of the transition through the successful completion of the installation of the new executive.

Composition. Ideally, the transition committee is a small team of five or so people — usually no more than seven if it is also serving the role of the search committee. Larger, more complex organizations may require larger transition committees of up to 10 people or more. The transition committee should include past, current, and prospective future board leaders. Many organizations include a senior member of the staff on the committee, but this person should not be a prospective candidate for the chief executive position. In these instances, the staff member usually is not involved in interviews, especially the final interview, nor in selection deliberations when the board needs to speak very frankly about the finalists' merits.

Structure. In most cases, the board chair or another officer chairs the committee. It is advisable for the transition committee to also serve as the search committee. In cases where the transition is complex and the transition committee faces a complicated set of duties, a larger transition committee might be advisable and a subset may be designated as the search committee. Similarly, some organizations parcel out the transition committee's work to various subcommittees (e.g., search, interviews, etc.) in order to provide broader involvement among the board. Increased inclusiveness is a worthy goal, but more complex structures usually require more effort to coordinate and to facilitate effective communication. In most cases, a simpler structure is better.

Responsibilities. The transition committee has five key responsibilities:

1. **Planning and overseeing communications with internal and external stakeholders.** The committee should make sure that the incumbent executive's departure is appropriately announced and that there is a plan in place for announcing the appointment of the incoming executive.

2. **Ensuring healthy closure with the departing executive and clarifying that person's role in the transition process.** The committee is responsible for appropriate acknowledgment of the departing executive's contributions, such as

a farewell ceremony that celebrates the individual's accomplishments and that allows staff and board to come to terms with the loss of this leader.

3. **Planning the hiring and transition activities.** The committee contracts with outside consultants to support the search and transition process; recruits an interim executive, as needed; and arranges for the transfer of duties between the departing executive and an interim executive (if appropriate) and, ultimately, the new chief executive. The committee also works to ensure that the transition is based on a solid action plan; that the board understands the organization's current status, including its strengths, challenges, and opportunities; and that any legacy issues are identified and that a plan is in place to address them. A key priority for the committee: helping the board clarify the organization's present and future leadership needs and articulate those in a profile of skills and characteristics needed in the next executive.

4. **Managing the hiring and transition process.** The committee executes a search plan and oversees any outside consultants. In this capacity, the committee plays a hands-on role in executing the search by placing all advertising and conducting outreach that yields a diverse candidate pool, screening resumes, arranging and conducting interviews, checking references, forwarding a finalist to the board for consideration, and negotiating the terms of employment with the selected executive.

5. **Providing a healthy start for the new executive.** The committee is responsible for articulating and securing board approval for short-term priorities for the first 12 to 18 months of the new executive's tenure. Among the other responsibilities at this stage: providing the executive with an orientation to the organization's programs, systems, people, and stakeholders; arranging for professional development and mentoring for the new executive, if needed; and planning the initial performance evaluation.

SORTING OUT ROLES BETWEEN THE BOARD CHAIR AND TRANSITION COMMITTEE CHAIR

In many organizations, the board chair winds up as transition committee chair as well. In some cases, this works just fine. But a better approach in most cases is for the transition committee to be led by someone else — ideally a current or past officer of the board who has a high level of familiarity with the organization. The board chair then can serve as an ex officio member of the transition committee. This allows the board chair to keep track of the process and take part in crucial discussions, without having to manage the day-to-day aspects of the transition. While the transition committee chair will be deeply involved in planning for the transition and overseeing the search and hiring process, the board chair will step up involvement after the hire. The focus of the board chair's post-hire work: building a strong working relationship with the new executive.

Transition Leadership: The Departing Chief Executive

The departing chief executive should focus on leading and managing the organization, not leading the transition. If the departing executive manages the process, the result will likely be a reflection of that person's thinking and vision for the organization, not the board's. Boards should specifically avoid situations in which the departing executive appoints or anoints a successor. The reason: The success of the organization hinges on the relationship between the board and the executive.

There are definite and important roles for the departing executive in grooming internal talent, giving staff diverse responsibilities that round out their skills and self-efficacy, providing opportunities for meaningful face time with the board, and highlighting their achievements. However, when it comes to the actual decision, the board needs to have its own self-defined process in place. A departing executive who cajoles the board into accepting a handpicked successor is a recipe for trouble.

Does this mean the departing executive should play no role in the transition at all? Of course not. Typically, the departing executive supports the transition process through a range of activities and responsibilities, such as

- *Preparing the platform for the successor.* This may include strengthening the organization's financial position, staff, and systems, and helping to strengthen the board.

- *Acting as a key information resource during the planning and execution of the search and selection.* This may include taking part in the planning work leading up to the search, meeting with the finalists to answer questions, and providing information that will help them and the board make a better choice. However, the departing executive should not sit in on interviews.

- *Ensuring a successful handoff to the incoming executive.* This may include working with the transition committee to plan the orientation process for the new executive; consulting with the new executive on the handoff; and proactively handing off key relationships, particularly those with donors.

In some cases, the departing executive can continue to play a role in the process even after the successor has been hired. However, the board needs to make absolutely sure that a departing executive actually departs and only returns to offer advice and guidance if asked.

Organizations often find it valuable to have an ongoing relationship with the departing executive — for example, by signing a consulting contract that makes the departing executive available as a resource to the new executive for a short time. The succeeding executive must be in charge of the relationship, however. Typically, there is a huge power differential between the departing and incoming executives at the early stage of the new executive's tenure. The board does not want to have a situation in which the power shadow of the departing executive usurps the authority of the successor.

For the same reason, it is typically a bad idea to invite the departing executive onto the board, at least right away. People need time to disengage from the departing executive and align with the new executive. Having the departing executive give up the responsibilities of the chief executive position and move into a programmatic or fundraising leadership role can be similarly problematic. This should only be done with ample assurances and understandings that the new executive has the ultimate authority over the predecessor's new role.

Regardless of how the ongoing relationship is structured, it is highly advisable that the departing executive take at least a short sabbatical before assuming any new role with the organization. This gives people a chance to bond with the new executive and sends a message to the outside world about the change in leadership.

Working with Consultants

Executive transitions can be difficult to manage. They are time-consuming and require a broad range of skills. Ideally, the transition committee should be appointed with an eye to including leaders who have prior experience in hiring executives or in human resources. If lacking these skills on the board, an organization might be well served to consider retaining a consultant who can bring expertise, time, and ready contacts to help the board meet the challenge.

Organizations facing executive transitions generally retain one of three types of consulting help:

1. Specialty consultants with subject-matter expertise and skills in strategic planning, board development, human resources, and other areas identified as priorities for the organization during the transition

2. Executive transition consultants who marry expertise in transition management and planning with the capacity to conduct an executive search

3. Executive search consultants who focus exclusively on helping organizations find a new chief executive

An organization's decision about which type of consulting help it needs — and whether it needs outside help at all — will depend on an honest assessment of the situation by the transition committee and the larger board.

If the board feels confident in its ability to manage the transition process but wants help sourcing candidates for the executive job, then the obvious choice is to go with a search consultant. On the other hand, if the organization is facing a challenging transition and wants help managing the process in a coordinated way, then it might consider working with an executive transition consultant. A specialty consultant may be just the ticket if the board feels it is capable of managing the transition and search but needs help with planning or human resources or other issues.

Most search and executive transition consultants work with nonprofit organizations on a retainer basis — billing the organization for their work on a monthly basis.

STAFF CHANGES DURING THE TRANSITION

Preparing the staff to work successfully under a new executive is a crucial part of the transition. In some cases, the staff preparation may involve personnel changes — terminations and/or new appointments. Generally, it's a good idea to minimize personnel changes during a transition to those that are absolutely necessary.

Terminations during the transition period are some of the most difficult of all transition matters and should be approached with extra care and sensitivity. Transitions are a time of high anxiety for the staff. A termination, however justified, can heighten those anxieties if poorly handled.

A critical question in many transitions is whether to fill key vacancies during the transition or wait until the new executive comes on board. If the staff position is part of the management team or one of the chief executive's direct reports, the best approach is usually to allow the new executive to make the hire. The board should therefore look at how it can cover the vacancy using an interim hire or an external contractor, or redeployment of current staff. If it is a mission-critical position, the board can further expedite the process by advertising the position and building a candidate pool simultaneously with the chief executive search and then allowing the final decision to be among the first that the new executive makes.

CONCLUSION

The board needs to take complete responsibility for the executive transition and not delegate leadership duties to its departing chief executive. The departing executive's role should be to lead the organization and be an adviser to the board and transition committee, but that person should not dominate or control the process. The bulk of the work will be done by the transition committee — a committee that is charged with addressing all of the crucial elements that make for a successful executive transition, including the hiring process.

5.

Acting and Interim Chief Executives

Organizations have two basic options when it comes to ensuring executive leadership during the transition. Either the departing executive stays in the position throughout the transition and hands the reins to a successor, or the departing executive leaves before the successor is appointed and the executive leadership role is filled by someone else. Typically, this involves appointing an acting or interim chief executive. This publication uses the umbrella term "temporary executive" to refer to both acting and interim executives.

When considering whether an organization could benefit from having a temporary executive, the board should consider the transition timeline. Is there likely to be a gap in the executive position? Are the departing executive's plans going to allow for an orderly handoff between that person and the successor? Is the timeline for the current executive's departure such that the board is feeling undue pressure and is likely to act hastily?

The appointment of an acting or interim chief executive can help provide the board with the breathing space it needs to pursue a more thorough search and make a more thoughtful choice about the next executive. As discussed earlier in this book, unnecessary urgency can lead to hasty decisions that may not be in the long-term interest of the organization.

This chapter describes the options before the board as it considers appointing or hiring a temporary executive, as well as what to look for in terms of skills and qualifications, where to find candidates for the job, and how to go about negotiating a contract.

OPTIONS FOR COVERING THE EXECUTIVE ROLE

Organizations generally turn to one of the following approaches for ensuring temporary coverage of the chief executive's role:

- **Acting chief executive** — This is usually a senior manager or other insider who is appointed to provide bridge management during the interim period. Typically, this manager serves in the acting capacity for four to six months during the planning and execution of the executive search. In larger organizations, the person serving in the deputy chief executive or chief operating officer position often is elevated to the acting chief executive role. The acting executive typically will go back to the previous role on the staff when a new chief executive is appointed. In some cases, the acting executive is a candidate for the permanent position. The board normally will make a temporary salary adjustment equivalent to the beginning of the chief executive's salary range in recognition that the acting chief executive has taken on additional responsibilities.

- **Interim chief executive** — This is typically a seasoned executive from outside the organization who, like the acting chief executive, provides bridge leadership. However, an important responsibility of the interim executive is to help prepare the organization to work more effectively with the incoming permanent executive. A good interim executive deals with the day-to-day affairs of the organization, while at the same time building the platform for the permanent successor. In this role, the interim executive helps the organization deal with political, system, staffing, leadership, or other capacity issues that, if not attended to, may divert the energies and attention of the new executive. Like the acting chief executive, the interim executive usually serves in this capacity for the four to six months that it typically takes to plan and execute an executive search. Interim executives often are former chief executives who are retired or who may have a consulting practice. They find getting back into the leadership fray for a short period to be both stimulating and rewarding. As a rule, the interim executive should not be a candidate for the permanent position.

- **Transition chief executive** — This is an executive from inside or outside the organization who is appointed for an extended period, often 12 to 24 months or more. The transition chief executive's job is to turn around an organization experiencing serious problems or to realign an underperforming organization. This approach is not nearly as common as the appointment of an acting or interim executive for a shorter term, but it can be a good strategy in the right circumstances and with the right leader.

- **Other options** — Of course, nothing says organizations have to adopt one of the three approaches outlined above. Other options for ensuring bridge leadership for the organization include making no change based on the assumption that the staff can continue without a chief executive officer for a limited period, bringing in a board member to lead the organization on a temporary basis, or creating a management team of senior staff members who are collectively responsible for leading the organization until a new chief executive comes on board.

Which approach should you use? The answer to this question can depend on a number of factors. These include an organization's management bench strength — i.e., the capacity of one or more senior managers to assume the leadership role. Another consideration is the nature of the chief executive job — How much of a grind is it? What are the demands facing the organization in the months ahead? And what kind of leadership does it need to meet those demands? Last but not least, boards should consider the nature of the transition facing the organization as they weigh what kind of temporary leadership might be required. (See Chapter 2 for the major transition types.)

A stable organization with a strong management team and a skilled deputy director may have the ideal conditions in place for appointing an acting executive. Conversely, an organization facing financial, systems, human resource, or political challenges could benefit from hiring an experienced former chief executive as an interim executive.

ROLES AND RESPONSIBILITIES OF THE TEMPORARY EXECUTIVE

The temporary chief executive's job usually entails two roles: first, providing day-to-day, bridge leadership and management for the organization, effectively bridging between two permanent executives; and second, getting the organization ready to work more effectively with the incoming permanent chief executive.

Bridge leadership. The bridge leadership and day-to-day management role involves the standard set of chief executive responsibilities:

- supporting the work of the board

- supervising and supporting the staff

- providing appropriate leadership and management for programs

- providing appropriate management of and involvement in fundraising

- overseeing the organization's finances and budget process

Transition leadership. The second role of the temporary executive, setting the stage for the permanent successor, is unique to the transition. It typically involves a set of specialized tasks and activities that are closely connected to the work of the board's transition committee or an external executive search/transition consultant. These specialized tasks may involve one or more of the following:

- bringing focus, clarity, and a forward vision to a situation that always involves varying degrees of anxiety and confusion

- working collaboratively on key legacy issues with the transition committee and transition consultant (if appropriate)

- managing a stepped-up communications effort relating to the transition

- providing assurance to wary stakeholders, particularly funders

- potentially renewing or recovering relationships with stakeholders who may have strayed from the organization during the previous executive's tenure

- dealing with any information and/or management deficiencies, particularly anything relating to finances, grants, and contract commitments, and other external/legal obligations

- helping to implement board-approved changes that will strengthen the capacity of the organization

- preparing the staff to build a good relationship with a new executive

- helping to plan the announcement, orientation, and launch of the new executive

- conducting an appropriate handoff process with the incoming executive

Special roles of the interim chief executive. Contracting with an external interim executive who brings high-level skills and expertise to the organization can help the board tackle unique challenges related to the transition. In the right situation, the interim chief executive can potentially provide important benefits to the organization, such as

- conducting an organizational review or assessment that leads to greater clarity about strengths, weaknesses, challenges, and opportunities facing the organization and its new executive

- helping the board clarify its vision and related present and future leadership needs for the organization

- modeling appropriate executive behavior for the staff and board if the departing executive wasn't a particularly skilled or effective leader

- helping the organization come to terms with its history, focusing attention on building on the organization's strengths while addressing weaknesses

- providing the incoming executive with a skilled, knowledgeable mentor for the handoff process

Often, boards make the decision about an interim vs. an acting chief executive based on availability of and familiarity with the people involved. A better approach is to consider objective factors like those outlined above, and to make the choice based on organizational needs and skill requirements, even if that means conducting a search for an interim executive.

KEY QUALIFICATIONS OF AN INTERIM CHIEF EXECUTIVE

- Has sufficient experience to assume the chief executive role

- Provides a non-anxious presence in the midst of transition, potentially a period of grief and/or conflict

- Is clear about own identity and role to facilitate the organization's mission

- Is willing to prepare the way for the successor

- Is aware of being a significant but limited or temporary part of the organization's history (not in it for own agenda)

- Is able to honor the work of others, past and present

- Is able to join the organization quickly and with ease

- Is able to diagnose the situation accurately and develop action plans quickly

- Is able to provide honest and accurate feedback

- Is clear about not being a candidate for the permanent position

HIRING OR APPOINTING A TEMPORARY EXECUTIVE

Before the board names a temporary chief executive, it must define the proper role and responsibilities for the position. Usually, defining the job of the interim or acting executive falls to the transition or executive committee, but members of these committees should not take this on in isolation. An important source of guidance and good perspective is the organization's management team and other staff. Often, the staff has a much more detailed picture of the organization's operations, challenges, and needs than the board.

Beginning with the end in mind, the board should ask first what it wants and needs the temporary executive to help the organization accomplish during the interim period. What's critical to success — for the organization and the transition — over the next few months?

Second, the board should review the current chief executive's job description with several questions in mind, such as

- What are the parts of this job (i.e., roles and responsibilities) that need to be elevated during this time of transition?

- Which parts of the job, if any, can be held at bay until the new permanent executive is appointed?

- Are there items on the organizational calendar — such as annual fundraising events or renewal of major grants — that will influence the acting or interim executive's role?

- Are there other urgent issues or challenges facing the organization right now?

The board also should consider whether there are legacy issues that need to be addressed during the interim period. Does the organization's financial information system need an upgrade? Is the HR system up to snuff? Does the board need training and development before it is truly ready to partner in a powerful way with a new permanent chief executive? These types of legacy issues can be difficult to address without a permanent chief executive. However, to the extent that the board and the temporary executive are able to identify these issues and start shaping solutions during the interim period, then it will create a more solid working platform for the incoming permanent executive. (See Chapter 2 for more on defining the organization's legacy issues and identifying key priorities that need to be addressed during the interim period.)

More often than not, the temporary chief executive role is internally focused. Unless transition priorities dictate otherwise, the acting or interim executive typically does not engage in high-visibility external activities to the same degree that might be expected of a permanent leader. However, there are very few absolutes in this work. For example, an organization's fundraising plan may require the chief executive to play a visible role, regardless of whether that person is in a temporary or permanent position. The temporary chief executive needs to do what's right for the organization without using the position as an opportunity to build or burnish a public profile.

WHERE TO LOOK FOR AN INTERIM CHIEF EXECUTIVE

In many larger cities and within some nonprofit networks, there are growing formal and informal pools of interim executives. Most municipalities also have a robust base of nonprofit consultants, many of whom are former chief executives. This consultant network is a rich resource for finding an interim executive.

For most community-based nonprofits, the most productive way to tap into this network is to start with local networks first — including the local nonprofit management support organization, the association of grantmakers in the area, and nonprofit degree programs at area colleges. Other great resources are statewide associations of nonprofits and affinity groups in the organization's program areas — e.g., associations of community mental health providers, regional arts associations, or environmental education associations. (For a list of statewide nonprofit associations, see the National Council of Nonprofit Associations Web site: www.ncna.org.)

Finally, the Alliance for Nonprofit Management, a national association of individual consultants and management assistance organizations focused on the nonprofit sector, has a searchable database on its Web site, www.allianceonline.org, where organizations can connect with local consultants.

THE INTERIM CHIEF EXECUTIVE JOB ANNOUNCEMENT

If an organization is hiring externally, it will need to develop a job announcement for the interim chief executive, typically one or two pages that cover the following:

- description of the organization

- brief description of the interim executive's role (bullet points)

- priorities or special tasks for the interim period

- duration of the appointment

- where to go for additional information (typically the organization's Web site)

- how to apply

TIPS FOR FINDING THE RIGHT PERSON FOR THE TEMPORARY EXECUTIVE ROLE

The following are some key points for boards to consider when hiring or appointing a temporary chief executive:

- **Look for management experience, not just familiarity with the organization's programs.** The interim chief executive's role is not a job-training opportunity. Typically, the most successful interim executives are mid- to late-career professionals. Management experience is paramount, while experience in the organization's particular program area is probably less essential.

- **Don't look through the same lens the board will use for the permanent executive's position.** Look for a match between experience and transition priorities. If, for example, the organization is laboring under an inadequate financial information system, the board may want to look for a temporary executive who has particular strength in that area, while also offering the capacity to bridge the leadership/management role.

- **Consider cultural competency.** Boards should consider hiring an interim executive whose background and demographic profile reflect the community served by the organization. Such an individual can bring cultural competency and important insights to the organization that can help ensure the success of the transition.

- **Look for a leadership style that matches the dynamics of the transition.** Successful interim executives tend to be action oriented but collaborative in their approach, with well-honed listening skills. They help the organization pursue its change agenda, but always in close collaboration with the board and in consultation with the staff. The interim period typically is not a time to take on bold new initiatives, nor is it a time for the interim executive to pursue that person's solo agenda or vision for the organization.

- **Look for flexibility.** Executive searches often take longer than anticipated. Boards should ensure that the interim chief executive is available beyond what may be an optimistic timeline.

- **Think twice before appointing a board member as the acting or interim executive.** Sometimes a board member will throw a hat into the ring, or the board will actively seek the candidacy of a board member believed to have the time and interest to lead the organization on a temporary basis. But, as the board considers what it needs in a temporary executive, familiarity with the organization should not supersede the executive skills needed to manage and lead during a time of transition.

GETTING TO A CONTRACT: KEY CONSIDERATIONS

The following are some contracting rules of thumb gleaned from the author's experience as a consultant with TransitionGuides and from the executive transitions work of CompassPoint Nonprofit Services in San Francisco.

- **Part-time versus full-time.** Most of the interim executives working with TransitionGuides and CompassPoint work part time, typically at least eight hours a week and usually not more than 32 hours a week; 20 to 24 hours a week is the average. There are several reasons to make the interim chief executive job a part-time role. First, the board typically is not asking the interim executive to engage in the broad range of activities that might be included in the permanent role. Second, interim executives often are consultants who have active practices to maintain. Third, the interim executive may be an independent contractor and would not be entitled to the organization's employee benefit package — including sick leave, vacation, and holidays.

- **Hourly versus flat rate.** The bulk of the interim executives working with TransitionGuides charge by the hour, but some prefer to contract for a set dollar figure monthly (or weekly) and agree to provide a certain number of hours for that figure.

- **Employee versus independent contractor.** The majority of the interim executives placed by TransitionGuides are independent contractors. They work under contract and receive a Form 1099 rather than a W-2. Some nonprofits, because of their particular legal circumstances or insurance requirements, have found it advisable or necessary to appoint the interim executive as a temporary employee. A board should consult its attorney and insurance professional to determine what's best for the organization.

- **Duration of the assignment.** If the board is contracting with the interim executive to provide leadership throughout the search planning and execution process, the assignment will probably last somewhere from four to six months. But, an organization's particular circumstances may require a shorter- or longer-term appointment. Whatever the circumstances, the board should be as clear as possible about the timeline before selecting and signing a contract with the interim executive. Boards also should include a contingency for ending the assignment early in the event that the search goes particularly well, or extending the assignment if the organization needs more time to develop an adequate candidate pool.

- **Contracts and work plans.** The contract with the interim chief executive can include a simple letter of agreement along with a detailed work plan (see Appendix 2). The work plan, which spells out the priorities for the interim period, is the heart and soul of the contract. It should clarify the work that needs to be done, the expectations of who's going to do what, and how to deal with contingencies.

GOVERNING WITH AN ACTING OR INTERIM EXECUTIVE IN PLACE

Organizational governance during a time of transition is not business as usual. Typically, the board's relationship with a temporary chief executive is different than it would be with a permanent leader. During the transition period, the board generally has a heightened need for information and for assurance that critical roles are being discharged, that key legacy issues are being addressed, and that things are on track for a successful handoff to a permanent executive down the line. As a result, the board-executive relationship may be characterized by a higher level of interaction and oversight during the interim period. The trick is not to let this heightened role for the board continue into the tenure of the permanent executive.

CONCLUSION

Every nonprofit organization going through a transition needs to clarify who's in charge. Appointing an interim or acting chief executive can provide the board with the breathing space it needs to make a good choice about the permanent executive and ensure that the organization is prepared to work more effectively with that new staff leader. Not every organization in transition will need an interim executive, but a good interim can be a powerful partner with the board to build the capacity of the organization during the transition period. Both research and practice demonstrate that groups that employ a skilled interim executive emerge from the transition as stronger organizations.

~ PART II CHECKLIST ~
MANAGING THE DEPARTURE AND TRANSITION

At this point in the process, the board has

✓ used the organize-stabilize-understand-plan-execute framework to ensure that the transition got off to a good start in the first five days

✓ developed and implemented a communications plan that ensures timely and effective outreach to stakeholders about the departure and initial transition plans

✓ announced the departure to staff and laid the groundwork for engaging staff as active partners in the work of the transition

✓ considered how the board itself may need to change in order to work more effectively with a new executive, and how to initiate those changes

✓ appointed a transition committee to plan and oversee the process on behalf of the board

✓ carved out an appropriate role for the departing executive in the transition, if leaving the organization on positive terms

✓ appointed or hired an acting or interim chief executive, or made other arrangements to ensure bridge leadership during the transition

✓ begun work to address legacy issues and otherwise prepare the organization for the arrival of a new permanent executive

Part III.

Managing the Search and Hiring Process

Questions answered in this part of the book:

What outreach tools and strategies can we use to make sure we attract a diverse pool of qualified candidates for the executive position?

What can we do to ensure a smooth process of candidate screening and selection, from resume management to interviews and reference checking?

What kinds of information do we need to provide to prospective candidates — and at what point in the process?

What procedures should we follow in making the job offer to our final choice?

What procedures should we follow to announce the appointment and ensure a successful start for the new executive?

6.

The Successful Search

As a result of the transition planning work outlined in previous chapters, the board should now have some clear impressions about the current and future leadership needs of the organization. The board also should have some insights about the mix of skills, experience, and leadership attributes that it is looking for in a new executive. The next step is to translate these impressions and insights into a position profile and the other materials needed to execute a search.

This chapter discusses how to move forward with a successful search and selection process.

GETTING STARTED: WHAT THE BOARD NEEDS

In order to initiate the search, the board needs to develop a detailed position profile, along with a compensation plan and search plan and budget.

A position profile is a three- to five-page document that presents essential information about the organization and the job. It begins with a brief organizational history followed by a summary description of the programs, staffing, governance, and finances. It typically also includes a description of the leadership position and provides an outline of the board's expectations of the new director. It concludes with information about how to apply. (See Appendix 3 for an example.)

The position profile serves multiple purposes. First, it ensures that the board has reached agreement internally about the nature of the job, the type of person it wants to hire, and the roles and responsibilities of the new executive. Second, the profile is a tool that the organization can use in its discussions with serious candidates. Third, it is a source document from which the board can extract the information for a more condensed position announcement that can be used in recruitment outreach, e-mails, on the organization's Web site, and elsewhere.

The compensation plan articulates the board's approved salary range (or at least its comfort zone) for the compensation package. It is based on compensation research to ensure that the organization is offering a competitive salary. Before an organization launches a search, the transition committee should review the compensation package and compare it to those offered by peer organizations. For points of reference, the committee can look to local and national salary and benefit surveys, state or national associations that the organization belongs to, the statewide association of nonprofits, and the local United Way. Other sources include reports by Abbott, Langer & Associates and Guidestar.org. Many of these studies can be reviewed for free at the Foundation Center's affiliate libraries (www.foundationcenter.org).

The search plan and budget is a short, two- to four-page document that outlines the strategies for developing the candidate pool, summarizes key search and selection activities, and includes a projected timetable. It should also include a board-approved budget that outlines the projected costs related to the search, such as advertising and Web posting costs, consultant fees, candidate travel reimbursements, and relocation stipend, if offered.

With these materials in hand, the organization is ready to begin the search and selection phase, which has three major steps: (1) recruiting a diverse candidate pool, (2) screening candidates and selecting a finalist, and (3) confirming the employment offer.

RECRUITING A DIVERSE CANDIDATE POOL

The recruitment process can involve a variety of tools, ranging from print advertising to Web site postings to direct contact with prospective candidates and with individuals who might help with candidate identification and recruitment. Among the most important priorities for the board as the process gets under way: achieving diversity of gender, race, and ethnicity among the candidates in the finalist pool.

The board should establish clear and explicit diversity goals to guide the transition committee in its work. This will help ensure that decisions about recruitment strategies reflect the board's goals. For example, as the committee considers ad placements for the position, it might broaden the advertising to include Spanish-language publications. Or, if the recruitment effort is reaching out to college alumni associations, the organization might want to target historically black colleges and universities.

Achieving a diverse finalist pool is not an accident; it requires a commitment by the organization's leaders to make diversity a priority and to make that priority clear to those who are managing the search and selection process.

Regardless of the organization's specific diversity goals, the recruitment effort will hinge on three key activities:

1. **Advertising.** Placing ads about the position is a reliable way to announce the organization's vacancy. Boards should start the recruiting process by placing ads first, because of the lead time between when the ad is placed and when it actually appears. Newspapers typically have the shortest lead times (two to three days), while national professional magazines and journals can have lead times extending to several months. The board will need to ensure that its search plan allows for this lead time and gives sufficient time for candidates to respond to ads.

2. **Web postings.** Online job announcements are an increasingly important part of the recruitment process. There are a variety of general job Web sites (e.g., Monster and CareerBuilder), as well as sites that are specific to the nonprofit sector (e.g., ExecSearches.com and Idealist.org). (See Appendix 4 for a list of potential Web sites where nonprofits can post their job announcements.) In addition to these general sites, boards should consider using job boards hosted by the statewide or national associations related to the organization's field of work.

3. **Direct recruitment.** Professional recruiters rely on direct recruitment to develop candidate pools for executive positions. This labor-intensive process involves making contact with a network of potential candidates and "nominators" who provide recruiters with ideas about possible candidates. A lone nonprofit may not be able to duplicate the depth of a recruiter's network, but every organization has its own base of contacts that can be successfully employed in the search for a new executive. Transition committee members will likely generate useful leads by spending just a few hours on the phone with leaders of allied or collaborating organizations, executives and officers of related statewide or national professional associations, and key program officers of interested foundations and corporate giving programs. This type of outreach is often the key to achieving a board's diversity goals for the finalist pool.

CANDIDATE SCREENING AND SELECTION

Once the organization's ads are out there, the announcement has been placed on the appropriate Web sites, and the board has made its recruitment calls, the resumes will (hopefully) start pouring in. Now, the search process moves to a new phase that includes a range of activities, from resume review through interviewing and making the offer.

Resume management. All resumes should come to one point of contact, whether they are received by fax, e-mail, or regular mail. This is an ideal task for a detail-oriented person with sufficient time to handle follow-through and record keeping. Typically, an organization will need to maintain the search records for at least two years and perhaps longer, depending on state laws.

The resume management process should include regularly checking for new resumes, keeping a log of the applicants, and forwarding resume copies to the person or team doing the resume review. The organization also should send an acknowledgment e-mail or note to candidates letting them know that their resumes have been received. Encouraging applicants to submit their resumes by e-mail makes the acknowledgment process much easier. Because a widely advertised e-mail address is going to be a target for spammers, the organization should consider setting up a disposable e-mail account on one of the free Web services rather than using a committee member's personal or business e-mail account.

If possible, the resume receipt and management process should take place outside of the organization's office — for example, in the office of a board member or the search consultant. All material submitted by the candidates should be considered confidential, including the fact that a candidate has applied for the position. Knowledge of the applicants should be limited to those people who really need to know. Typically, this includes only the members of the transition committee involved in the hiring process.

Resume review. This process usually involves one or more reviewers who read all of the resumes and sort them into categories. Based on the resume review, organizations should consider creating a three-tiered list of candidates as follows:

- A list — Candidates who meet all of the criteria. The experience outlined on the resume suggests that the candidate could clearly do the job.

- B list — Candidates who meet most of the criteria. The resume suggests that they might be suitable.

- C list — Candidates who do not meet the criteria or whose experience is clearly not up to the job.

See Appendix 5 for a sample resume-scoring sheet.

Candidate vetting and questionnaires. Organizations can consider a number of strategies and activities as a segue between the resume review and the interview process. The goal at this point might be to narrow an especially large pool of A-list candidates to a more manageable group of the most promising candidates that the organization wants to invite to interviews. Alternatively, the organization might want a better idea of which B-list candidates have the right stuff for the job. Vetting can consist of a committee member conducting a short phone interview with promising candidates using a few select questions, plus follow-up questions to cover items not addressed in the individual's resume. Another screening tool is a candidate questionnaire, ideally something that is short and can be sent and returned via e-mail. (See Appendix 6 for sample vetting questions.)

The vetting interview or questionnaire process can help the organization get a better idea of the depth and diversity of the candidate pool so the board can make a judgment about whether it is ready to proceed with interviews or whether additional recruitment is warranted. The screening interviews also should help determine if the salary expectations of the identified candidates fall within the organization's range. Finally, this process will help the organization gather information about the candidates' availability for interviews and how much notice they might need to give their current employers, as well as other factors that might affect their availability to join the organization.

Interviews. Candidate interviews should be a several-step process. The transition committee might hold a first round of interviews with five or six candidates, followed by round-two interviews with two or three semifinalists, and a round-three interview in which the finalist selected by the executive committee meets with the entire board. (See Appendix 7 for an interview agenda and a list of potential interview questions.) Ideally, at the conclusion of the second interview, the committee should have at least two good choices to move forward with, with a preferred candidate and an equally stellar and exciting alternate. (See Appendix 8 for sample interview rating criteria.) But boards should remember that candidates have been known to bow out at the 11th hour. Similarly, the board's pre-employment negotiations with the finalist could break down. Rather than having to revisit the search, ideally the organization has built a very strong candidate pool so it has multiple good candidates to choose from.

The interview process should include both formal and informal time for the finalists to meet with board and staff. This interaction will vary depending on the size and culture of the organization. The process might include a visit to the office and key facilities, meetings with staff or senior managers, social time with key board leaders and/or funders, among other possibilities. Staff involvement varies and minimally includes an opportunity for the finalists to meet with senior managers and with the outgoing chief executive, where appropriate. In other instances, one or two staff representatives will serve on the transition committee. Because there is a two-way sale between organization and candidate, interaction between staff and final candidates is important. Be careful, however: In some instances, candidates for the chief executive job may not want their current employers or others to know that they are interviewing for other positions. This may limit the ability of boards to engage staff in the interview process.

TIPS FOR SUCCESSFUL INTERVIEWS

- **The more interviews, the better.** Conducting a single interview with a top candidate for the executive job is not enough. Candidates should participate in multiple interviews as the field is winnowed down.

- **Watch the hypotheticals.** The best interview questions are "behaviorally based" — meaning they are intended to elicit a response that shows how the interviewee has responded to past situations or problems. Don't ask, "How would you handle X situation?" A better question: "Have you ever had an opportunity to do X? Tell me what you did, and why."

- **Create time for informal talk.** The interview process shouldn't focus solely on formal questioning regarding the candidate's qualifications. For candidates moving along in the process, it's important to organize opportunities for informal back-and-forth. Members of the transition committee may want to invite the candidate to lunch for a "get-to-know-me" conversation.

- **One-on-one is not enough.** The transition committee needs a shared sense of different candidates' qualifications for the position. This can mean conducting interviews in a committee setting, with two or more committee members guiding the questioning.

- **Keep to a set group of interviewers.** Having different people interviewing different candidates can confuse the process. A better approach is to have the same set of committee members seeing all candidates so they can draw common conclusions. One idea is to schedule all interviews in one day so committee members can see the candidates back-to-back.

- **Face time beats the phone.** While an initial phone interview may be necessary when considering nonlocal candidates for the executive position, face-to-face discussions are essential as the process moves along.

References and background checks. Checking a candidate's references is a crucial step in the selection process and is best done between the first and second round of interviews. Reference checks involve interviews with people who know the candidate. The committee will want to check at least three and as many as six references.

References should represent a range of views about the candidate — for example, someone who has supervised the candidate (ideally a board chair or board member at a previous nonprofit employer, if the candidate has been an executive before); someone whom the candidate has supervised; and a peer. (See Appendix 9 for sample reference checking tools.)

In contrast to reference checks, pre-employment background checks are contracted out to a firm that specializes in this work. The background check may involve one or more of the following: criminal background, credit history, education/license certification, and/or driving records. But the check should include only those items that are clearly warranted. For example, if the job involves contact with children, a check of the sexual predator registries would be required. Background checks are regulated by the Federal Trade Commission. The process must meet the requirements of the Fair Credit Reporting Act, and the candidate will have to sign a release before the contractor can conduct a background check. The firm conducting the background checks will have copies of the release and other supporting materials.

The offer. The job offer should precede the board ratification vote and employment confirmation. At this point, negotiations with the finalist should be at a point where all that remains is the signing of the pre-negotiated employment offer. Earlier in the process, at the vetting and interview stages or between the first and second interviews, the committee will want to have a very frank discussion with the most promising candidates about compensation so there aren't any surprises when things move to the negotiation stage. The goal should be to have an agreement in principle, subject to board ratification, completely ironed out before the finalist goes before the board.

The offer letter or contract. The conclusion of the interview process is a ratification vote by the board of directors. The bylaws of most nonprofits call for the board to hire the chief executive. Accordingly, a review of the candidate by the board and an affirmative vote by the board to extend an employment offer are crucial. The final step is to confirm the offer with an employment offer letter or an employment contract. The offer letter or contract should be a reflection of prior negotiations with the finalist about salary, benefits, and expectations. (See Appendix 10 for a sample employment offer letter.)

An employment offer can be a binding contract with many legal implications; legal counsel should therefore review it before it is forwarded to the finalist. Most nonprofits use an employment confirmation letter that identifies the starting salary, benefits (especially if they are different than those covered in the employee handbook), the reporting relationship, and any other conditions. In states that allow at-will employment, the letter should make clear that the employment relationship is at-will.

Employment contracts are more prevalent among larger nonprofits and trade associations. An employment contract typically spells out the same information as an offer letter, but covers a defined period of time (typically three years) and includes a termination clause that addresses severance pay. Drafting an employment contract is a job for legal counsel.

At this time, the organization also should send regrets letters to all candidates who submitted resumes and participated in interviews. (See Appendix 11 for samples.)

WHEN A CANDIDATE FOR THE EXECUTIVE JOB IS ON THE STAFF

The staff can be an organization's most valuable resource in an executive transition — both as a source of insights and guidance about what the organization needs in a new executive, and sometimes as a source of candidates for the job.

However, even when one or more members of the staff step up to express an interest in the executive position, boards are well advised to embark on a competitive search that weighs the merits of a range of internal and external candidates. Only then will the board have full confidence that it has conducted the necessary due diligence and found the best possible person for the job.

When considering internal candidates for the executive job, the board should exercise great care. These are usually people with a great investment in the organization — they have worked there for some time, they believe deeply in its mission and are committed to its success. The board needs to recognize and honor their commitment — not by granting them special consideration over and above other candidates who might be more qualified for the job, but by treating staff candidates seriously and with the utmost respect.

For example, while the organization might simply send a letter or e-mail to external candidates removed from consideration at the resume review stage, staff candidates in the same situation should receive a phone call from the transition committee chair or other board official. The goals of the call: to explain the reasons for the decision, while expressing the board's sincere hope that the individual will continue as an asset to the organization.

Boards often wonder whether they should interview all internal candidates for the chief executive job regardless of their qualifications. The answer is a firm "No." Internal candidates for the position should move forward in the process because of their merit and not for political reasons.

DECIDING WHAT INFORMATION TO PROVIDE TO CANDIDATES

Boards are often somewhat hesitant about sharing information because they are not sure how much to disclose and when. There's a natural tendency to not "air the linens." But the fact is that good information and a positive attitude toward disclosure can go a long way toward ensuring that candidates understand what they are getting into, and that they are ready to lead the organization from day one. Being transparent with the candidates during the interview process will help avoid disappointment later on.

The board should make sure that all serious candidates for the job are provided with substantive briefing materials about the organization and about the position they may ultimately assume. These "disclosures" should be staged based on what information is needed at each point in the hiring process.

Generally, two sets of briefing packages should be given to candidates during the interview phase as follows:

Package #1. This is supplied prior to the first round of interviews, and is typically included with the mailing of the interview confirmation letter. This package contains the sort of general information that would facilitate an informed conversation during this "first-date" meeting. The package includes

1. Position announcement and/or job description

2. Web site address

3. If no Web site or the Web site has limited information, consider mailing/ e-mailing the following:

    a. organizational brochure

    b. last annual report (if published)

    c. latest newsletter

    d. brochures or fact sheets on major programs

    e. any other materials the organization might provide to a prospective member or donor

Package #2. This is supplied to the finalists before the final interview with the board or executive committee. This package, which is considerably more comprehensive, is designed to accomplish two things: (1) it allows the candidates to do their due diligence research prior to being offered the assignment, and (2) it provides the information base that the finalists will use to develop the "strategic challenges and opportunities" presentation that is an integral part of final selection interviews. This package includes

1. General (as a supplement to the information supplied in Package #1)

    a. annual reports from two previous years (if published)

    b. recent back issues of the newsletters/journal, etc.

    c. information about membership or donor categories

    d. a list of any publications

    e. information about any existing or proposed formal coalitions, joint ventures, etc.

2. Governance, policies, and direction

    a. board list (with bios if available)

b. bylaws

c. major policies that are directly relevant to the position, e.g., board governance policies, etc.

d. information about the relationship of any chapter and subsidiary organizations

e. strategic and/or business plan

f. executive summary section of any recent needs assessment reports

g. executive summary section of any recent management studies

3. Financial

a. last two audits (three if there are major fluctuations)

b. current year budget

c. most recent year-to-date financial statement

d. cash flow projection (if available)

e. data on membership and/or donor growth or decline

4. Personnel/Operations

a. staff and board organization charts (if available)

b. list of staff, positions, and tenure (bios if they are available)

c. employee benefit schedule

d. personnel policies

e. information about major operational contractors, e.g., external fundraisers, major service delivery contractors, etc.

f. information about staff turnover

g. disclosure about any ongoing or proposed contracts (or other relationships) with the previous chief executive(s) or any current or past officers

PRE-HIRE DISCLOSURE

The following items generally are not part of the information packages provided to prospective candidates for the chief executive job because they may contain sensitive and proprietary information. If relevant, however, this information should be conveyed to the candidates in writing prior to the final interview:

1. Results of any recent or ongoing merger or acquisition discussions. This information usually is discussed in general terms during the first round of interviews. If a merger is pending, it can be discussed in depth prior to the final interview.

2. Disclosure of any pending lawsuits

3. Disclosure of any pending or recent regulatory actions — e.g., IRS, OSHA, DOL, or other federal or state actions

4. Disclosure of any pending or recent actions by the organization's sanctioning or accrediting bodies — e.g., health care facility recertification, etc.

5. Delineation of check- and contract-signing authority as well as personnel hiring and discharge authority

CONCLUSION

The search process is where the rubber meets the road in an executive transition. All of the organization's planning, as well as all of its hard thinking about the future and the kind of leadership it needs, will now come to a head as the board sets out to find the best candidate for the chief executive job. A successful search requires the board to always refer back to the goals and vision laid out earlier in the transition process. An organization may never find the "perfect candidate" for the job, but the board should not compromise as it looks for someone with the fundamental skills and qualifications that are required to stabilize the organization and create a successful future.

7.

After the Hire: Launching and Keeping the New Executive

Now the search is complete and all of the people involved — board and staff — are ready to breathe a sigh of relief and get back to business as usual. This is a natural inclination. Once the new executive is on board, everybody is excited about the future. People also may be tired, perhaps even exhausted, after the search process.

But there is still work to do to ensure that the new executive has a successful start. The board and organization have made a significant investment in finding a new executive. The post-hire process is about making the most of that investment.

At a minimum, board members should ask themselves three questions:

- What can we do to help our new executive to start on the right foot?

- What can we do to structure the board-executive relationship in a positive way?

- What can we do to make sure we achieve the priorities we identified in the planning stage of this transition?

This chapter offers a step-by-step approach to setting the stage for both the executive and the organization to thrive.

ANNOUNCE THE APPOINTMENT

The new executive's appointment will be of interest to a range of stakeholders in the organization's work, from clients and community members to major donors and the press. Planning the announcement involves targeting the organization's audiences, identifying the vehicles to reach those audiences, and developing messages and materials for the announcement.

The basic materials and strategies an organization will use to announce the appointment are similar to those used to announce the departure of the previous executive (see Chapter 3). At a minimum, the materials might include the following: a press release, biography of the new executive, a letter to stakeholders, and a photo of the new executive (for the press). As in the case of the departure, the list of contacts should be segmented into those who should receive a phone call, those who should receive a letter, and those who will read about the appointment in the newsletter.

The announcement of a new chief executive is an opportunity to do more than simply tout the incoming leader's credentials. It is also a chance for the board to signal a new direction or vision for the organization, particularly for those organizations that are making a significant pivot or change with this transition.

Similarly, the announcement can be an opportunity to create further alignment and buy-in among key stakeholders in the organization's success.

The responsibility for planning the announcement falls on the transition committee, although there typically will be a lot of overlap with the staff.

CREATE A SOLID ORIENTATION

The orientation process typically begins with a solid briefing for the new chief executive. During the briefing, the board can once again go over the information provided prior to the second interview regarding organizational structure, systems, staffing, board, and finances. If the organization covers an extended geographic area or has dispersed facilities, the orientation process might include a tour of those facilities and a meeting with key staff. If it's a membership organization, the orientation might include the incoming executive going on a listening tour to hear what's on the minds of members. Boards should think creatively about what would be the most complete, empowering orientation they can provide for the incoming executive.

Preparations for the executive's orientation should begin in earnest after the new executive has been identified and has a general start date. A simple, one- to two-page orientation plan will help the board think through the key points to be covered in the orientation and identify the participants and their assignments.

Typically, the orientation will include a series of briefings or discussions rather than a brain dump by one individual. Potential topics and participants for the orientation include

- **Strategic direction and key external issues.** This includes discussion of the organization's strategic direction and long-range plan. Ideally, the strategic or long-range plan was shared with the candidates during the interview phase. Often, the discussion of strategic direction can be combined with a dialog about current external issues facing the organization as well as those on the horizon. Participants: board chair, planning committee chair, executive committee, key staff.

- **Financial and legal review.** This includes review of the current financial status, as well as any legal issues facing the organization. Participants: key financial staff, treasurer, external accountant, and legal counsel (if appropriate).

- **Funding outlook.** This includes a review of current fund development plans, activities, projected net revenues, etc. Participants: key development and financial staff, fundraising committee chair.

- **Program status and outcomes.** This includes in-depth discussion about the status of programs and any outcome or evaluation data. Briefings might include visits to off-site facilities and meetings with leaders of constituent groups, if applicable. Participants: program directors.

- **Board.** This includes dialog about board issues and the status of board development. Participants: executive committee or board development chair and board chair.

- **Staffing.** This includes discussion of any key staff vacancies, human resource issues, status of personnel reviews, etc. Participants: director of human resources and/or other staff member who has handled employment files (if applicable).

- **Other.** Depending on the organization's situation, other topics that might be important to cover in briefings include marketing, volunteers, systems, facilities, and information technology.

Obviously, the size of the organization and the dynamics of the situation will affect the structure of the orientation process. In small organizations, these discussions might be combined into one or two conversations. In large organizations, the briefing process will likely be more extensive. The departing executive might also be a participant in these discussions, depending on the departure circumstances and timing.

Where possible, a briefing book of key documents and an index of where to find contracts, grant agreements, personnel files, and other information will be quite helpful for the new executive. If the organization had an interim executive in place, assembling the briefing book and going over it with incoming executive is often one of that person's final handoff tasks.

START BUILDING RELATIONSHIPS EARLY

The new chief executive should be strongly encouraged to make personal contact with all key stakeholders as early as possible. This means meeting with as many staff members as possible in the first day or two on the job, and reaching out to board members through personal visits or phone calls during the first two weeks.

Another crucial group of stakeholders includes the organization's contributors and foundation supporters. The staff and leaders of foundations that support the organization will expect to hear from the new executive as early as possible, particularly if the foundation has made substantial investments in the organization. If foundations and individual donors have established a trusting relationship with the departing leader, they will be comforted to see that person make an implied endorsement of the new executive through a joint meeting or similar handoff of the relationship. Boards should consider providing for sufficient overlap between the departing and incoming executives so that these crucial relationships can be transferred appropriately. Keep in mind the old adage that people give money to people, not organizations.

Meeting the New Executive's Informational Needs

Once on board, the new chief executive will likely want to review many of the following items as part of the orientation and "settling-in" process. At a minimum, the executive may simply want assurance that the file or item exists and can be located when needed.

1. Articles of incorporation

2. Form 1023 (Application for Exempt Status) and the exempt status determination letter from the IRS

3. Board and committee minute files

4. Tax and regulatory filings:

   a. Form 990 file

   b. State income report filings (if relevant)

   c. Proof of payment of federal and state employee withholding

   d. Proof of payment of Unrelated Business Income taxes

   e. State charitable solicitation registration and report filings

   f. Other tax or regulatory filings

   g. Organization's status regarding property and sales taxes

5. Financial:

   a. Information about accounting method (cash or accrual), systems(s), and methods used

   b. Responsibilities of employees involved in accounting/finances

   c. Current balance sheet and statement of activities

   d. Year-to-date (YTD) budget versus actual

   e. YTD comparison to last year

   f. Recent cash position and cash flow projection

   g. Receivable and payable aging schedules

   h. Reserve fund statements

   i. List of assets and depreciation schedule

   j. Information about line of credit

   k. Major leases

   l. Proof of account reconciliations

6. Audit file as well as the contract with the current auditor and history of the relationship with auditor

7. Key policies:

   a. Employee handbook or policy

   b. Board policy on investment of reserve funds

   c. Purchase and expense policy

   d. Policy on travel expense reimbursements for both staff and board plus related forms

   e. Other key policies or manuals

8. Contracts or memoranda of understanding with any subsidiary or umbrella organizations

9. Proof of insurance or actual insurance policies:

   a. Umbrella liability

   b. Directors & Officers liability insurance

   c. Professional liability/errors and omissions, if relevant

   d. Product liability, if relevant

   e. Employee bonds, if relevant

10. Recent correspondence between chief executive and the board

11. Job descriptions and resumes for all key employees and direct reports

12. List of key suppliers, products/services provided, and history

UNDERSTAND THE TAKING-CHARGE PROCESS

The process of fully settling into the top leadership role in an organization takes some time to complete. John Gabarro of The Harvard Business School has identified distinct phases of the taking-charge process that reflect the executive's education/assimilation into the organization and the organizational changes wrought by their leadership. The following chart lays out the stages, duration, critical actions and the impact on the organization based on my practice experience.

Stage and Duration	Action	Organizational Change
Entry — The first three to six months of the new executive's tenure.	New executive's introduction and orientation — early-stage learning and beginning to take the reins of the organization. Critical relationships are established. Executive assesses the organization, staff and board, etc.	Organizational changes can be numerous but are typically limited in scope, such as small, corrective actions and solving problems left over from the transition.
Immersion — An additional three to six months.	The executive is over the initial learning hump. Learning continues, but it's more "fine grained" and at a less hectic pace than during *Entry*. The executive begins to manage the organization in a more informed fashion.	Changes tend to be few during this stage. Later in this stage, executives often begin planning the actions that will take place in the *Reshaping* phase, either by revisiting the current strategic plan or instituting a new planning process.
Reshaping — Generally encompasses another three to six months.	Learning continues but at a slower pace. Implement the planning work begun during the *Immersion* phase.	Implementation of changes outlined in the planning work. Often this phase results in the most significant and strategic organizational changes to date.
Consolidation — variable.	Follow-through on the planning work.	Further implementation of the planning work and addressing the unintended consequences of some changes initiated during the *Reshaping* stage.
Refinement — ongoing.	The final phase in the taking-charge process. The executive is no longer considered new, and the job is no longer new to the executive.	The pace of change often slows down and involves ongoing refinement of operations and exploration of new opportunities.

Entry through *Reshaping* generally spans the first 12 to 18 months of a new executive's tenure. Earlier in the book, I stressed the importance of developing clear priorities for this critical period. Having well-honed, agreed on priorities for these early stages provides the executive with a sense of direction, clarity, and comfort from knowing that he/she is aligned with the board. This frees up the executive to focus on the critical actions in his/her taking-charge process.

Gabarro's research found that it takes two to three years to move through all five of the phases. However, it should be noted that Gabarro's work was completed in 1985. With the Internet and information technology now accelerating the pace of change for organizations and individuals, Gabarro's 36-month timeline may be more like 18 months or less today.

TransitionGuides has found that by the end of an executive's first complete budget cycle, most are deep into the work described in the *Reshaping* phase. At this time, they are working with the staff to pursue the objectives in the strategic plan that the executives inherited, or they are working with the board and staff in a new cycle of planning.

Get a Grip on Early Challenges. Within a few weeks, the initial excitement regarding the new executive's appointment will be over, and both the board and the executive will settle into the realities of organizational life and working together. Both the board and the executive face their own set of early challenges.

Challenges for the new executive. Every executive moving into a new position faces a similar set of challenges regardless of prior experience. The executive's challenges include

- gaining an understanding of the organization and acquiring knowledge — quickly

- figuring out who's who and establishing solid working relationships

- setting good priorities

- meeting pent-up demands for change

- making decisions that may have been deferred during the interim period

- managing expectations and negotiating competing demands

- building a support coalition to back needed changes

- balancing both organizational and personal transitions

Challenges for the board. Similarly, the board faces its own set of post-hire challenges. These include

- shifting gears after the search and finding the energy to address important relationship-building work

- effectively launching and supporting the new executive

- adjusting to the new executive's leadership style, as well as the executive's expectations and needs in relation to the board

- building trust with the new executive

- avoiding the dangerous polarities of micromanagement and excessive confidence

- avoiding savior thinking on the one hand — i.e., believing that the new executive will solve any and all problems — and dealing with buyer's remorse on the other

- ensuring that legacy issues and thinking ruts (e.g., "We've always done it that way") don't derail the work

It's critical that the board and executive avoid letting post-hire challenges reach a point where they derail the new executive's tenure. Good communications are essential for managing these challenges. The best post-hire situations are those where the board chair and executive are in frequent (weekly) contact about what's going on, breakthroughs and challenges, and the rate of progress against identified priorities.

IDENTIFY THE EXECUTIVE'S NEEDS AND PROVIDE SUPPORT

In almost all cases, the hiring process ends on a high note with the board enthusiastic about its choice of a new chief executive. This is a good thing, but sometimes this exuberance results in a false sense of reality. While the board should certainly extol the virtues of the new executive, it also should be realistic about the kinds of support the executive might need.

In all likelihood, there are areas where every new chief executive will want or need either support or professional development. Executives should think critically about their professional development and support needs and proactively seek out training, coaching, and other forms of support.

Boards should consider having the incoming chief executive prepare a 90-day entry plan. This is typically a short document (1–2 pages) that outlines how the new executive will tackle important learning needs, the relationship-building process with board and staff, and key short-term challenges. (See Appendix 12 for an example.) The entry plan is a good place to make notes about any support or professional development that the new executive might require. Entry planning is really a process of reflection and prioritization — it's a time to step out of the fray, reflect on what's ahead, and consider what it will take for the new executive to succeed in the first weeks on the job.

These initial weeks of a new executive's tenure are also a time for the board to reflect on areas for its own growth and development. During transition planning, the board may have identified some changes in practices and behavior that it would like to make in order to be a more effective partner with the new chief executive. The board chair and governance committee chair should ensure that those insights about board performance are translated into a developmental program for the board.

CREATE A "LEADERSHIP AGENDA" FOR THE ORGANIZATION

One of the most crucial relationships to the success of a nonprofit organization is the relationship, or social contract, between the board and the chief executive. As Barry Dym points out in *Leadership in Nonprofit Organizations*, the principal job of leadership is to create alignment between team behavior and the organization's strategic objectives.

Effective teams typically are aligned on a few strategic priorities or aims. To help bring clarity and focus to the early months of a new executive's tenure, the executive and the board should agree on a list of no more than six priorities that are crucial to success in the organization during this period. This list of key priorities is the leadership agenda for the organization — it's not the board's priority list nor is it a to-do list prepared exclusively by the chief executive. Rather, it is the result of a collaborative, back-and-forth discussion between the board and the executive.

The leadership agenda can then be used to monitor the organization's performance in the early months of the chief executive's tenure. During board meetings, the board can revisit the priorities from the leadership agenda and identify the next actions needed from the board or the executive to stay on track.

DEFINE HOW TO MONITOR PERFORMANCE

Boards should evaluate themselves frequently and the executive annually and discuss the results in the context of what changes are necessary for the organization's future success. The board and executive form two sides of the top leadership equation. Evaluating both sides of the equation gives the board a picture of the whole.

The executive's evaluation should be focused on overall organizational performance, the executive's contributions toward achievement of the priorities in the leadership agenda, and the executive's contributions toward building the health and vitality of the organization. An example of a measure used to evaluate the chief executive might be expanding the donor base from X to Y or reducing staff turnover from B percent to A percent.

There are a variety of good tools boards can use to evaluate themselves and their chief executives. The key is to focus not on role performance or behaviors but rather on impact on organizational outcomes.

The first year of a new executive's tenure requires a different set of evaluation tools and a different timetable than might be used in succeeding years. Typically, the board evaluates the chief executive's performance annually. During the first year, however, a graduated approach is in order. Here's a possible timeline:

SMART TRANSITIONS IN ACTION: SAFE PASSAGE

Safe Passage is an international nonprofit founded in 1999 that provides educational opportunities for at-risk children of families working in the Guatemala City garbage dump. The organization has board members across the country, a small development staff in Maine, a larger staff based in Guatemala, and 60 long-term volunteers. In 2007, Hanley Denning, the founding chief executive, died unexpectedly in a bus accident.

The organization didn't have a succession plan, and while many board members had been involved in Safe Passage for several years, the current board had been formed less than two years before. Up against considerable odds, the organization managed to execute a successful transition that included hiring a new chief executive in five months. Here's how they did it.

Immediately after learning of the executive's death, the board vice president and the board president personally called each of the 10 board members with the news. The next day, the board met by conference call to discuss next steps. The board unanimously agreed to appoint the chief financial officer as the interim chief executive and formed a transition committee that included five board members.

The transition committee met weekly by phone and began identifying the qualities the organization would need in its next chief executive. Transition committee members spent time in Guatemala so they could show support for the staff, volunteers, children, and families. In addition, committee members conducted interviews with staff to explore the current needs of the organization. (See Appendix 13 for an example of this type of interview.)

After talking with various executive search firms, the transition committee decided not to hire an external firm, but to manage the search itself. Committee members phoned or met with more than 200 individuals in Guatemala, the United States, and other countries, asking for names of good candidates, and then calling those individuals to inspire them to apply. The position was advertised internationally, and an asynchronous, online process was set up that enabled all committee members to participate in the review process.

Safe Passages received more than 75 applications for the position, and each was rated by at least two committee members using a predetermined scale. Applicants with one or more top ratings were asked to complete an additional questionnaire. After a series of phone interviews with the top candidates, along with reference checks, the committee selected three highly qualified finalists to invite to Guatemala for three days of interviews with staff, volunteers, board members, and parents. The interview visit ended with each candidate presenting to the transition committee a preliminary SWOT (Strengths, Weaknesses, Opportunities, Threats) analysis of the organization. After further reference checking and discussion, the board unanimously agreed to offer the position to Barbara Nijhuis, a young woman from Amsterdam who had founded a similar but smaller project in rural Guatemala. The transition committee recommended policies for assessing the organization's program and evaluating the new executive and the board.

At the same time that the search was proceeding, the board was involved in another aspect of the transition by updating the Safe Passage strategic plan based on the transition committee's review of the organization's operations. The board also amended the organization's bylaws to increase the size of the board and developed a fundraising plan that resulted in record donations.

Five months after the loss of the founder, Safe Passage welcomed its new chief executive. A representative of the transition committee spent six weeks in Guatemala to support the new executive by providing a sounding board; assisting in the planning process as requested by the executive; and gathering data about the organization into a fact book that showed enrollment, attendance, educational, financial, and staffing trends over time.

To provide ongoing support after the new executive's "settling-in" period, the board chair and the chair of the transition committee held a weekly conference call with the executive. At the end of the first six months, they also implemented an informal performance review to give the executive some early feedback. As the new executive neared the end of her first year leading Safe Passage, she and the board could point to several important accomplishments, including

- securing good placements for the children in the residential home

- creating a zero-based budget

- implementing a participatory planning process

- creating a rewarding work environment for staff and volunteers

- enhancing programs to help hundreds of students receive an education and social support

Out of a tragic accident, the Safe Passage board found the courage to make changes that it believes will ensure a bright future for the organization.

- After 90 days, an informal "how's it going" check-in to review progress against the 90-day entry plan.

- After six months, a slightly more formal review of the executive's progress on the taking-charge process — assuming the proper level of leadership and oversight for key aspects of the organization, such as fundraising, board support/development, etc.

- After 12 months, a formal review focused principally on the achievement of the executive's responsibilities for the items on the leadership agenda and contributions toward organizational performance. (This is usually a different review than the executive's annual, year-end performance review emphasizing organizational accomplishments. BoardSource's *Assessment of the Chief Executive: A Tool for Nonprofit Boards* is one good example of the year-end performance review.)

FOCUS ON RETENTION — RIGHT FROM THE START

Retaining a good executive can hinge on a variety of factors. A competitive compensation plan can go a long way, as can a retirement program. But, two huge and typically overlooked factors in executive retention are the board's support for the executive and the board's level of engagement in the organization.

One of the key findings from the 2006 *Daring to Lead* study is that executives who are unhappy with their boards are more than twice as likely to be planning near-term

SUPPORTING THE NEW CHIEF EXECUTIVE: KEY STEPS FOR THE BOARD

- Design and implement a thorough orientation.

- Ensure that the new executive has essential information and materials about the organization's finances, policies, and more.

- Arrange for introductions of the new executive at community forums, executive sessions with other nonprofit leaders, and other events.

- Join the new executive in personal visits and phone calls with key donors and organizational partners.

- Offer training, coaching, or other professional development opportunities for the new executive, as needed.

- Develop a 90-day entry plan for the new executive identifying key short-term challenges and opportunities, along with orientation and learning priorities.

- Work with the new executive to develop a leadership agenda for the organization identifying short-term strategic priorities.

- Develop a plan for monitoring the new executive's performance.

departures than those who have positive perceptions of their boards. The study outlines several specific board-related factors affecting executive perceptions and their tenure decisions:

- Board is not personally supportive.

- Board doesn't understand the chief executive's role.

- Board doesn't value the chief executive's contribution.

- Staff doesn't view the board as leaders.

The study goes on to point out that a major factor in chief executives' frustration with their boards is lack of support for fundraising. The *Daring to Lead* authors suggest that frustration about fundraising may be a marker for a more pernicious issue: low levels of board engagement.

Executive transitions are a time-consuming and expensive proposition, both in real costs and in the opportunity costs of having staff and board energy focused on the transition rather than the programmatic work of the organization. Clearly, the best course of action for a board to ensure a good return on this investment is to work to retain a great executive, and to help a good executive become a great one. As the *Daring to Lead* study suggests, one of the greatest impacts the board can have on executive tenure is to support and partner with the new chief executive to the greatest extent possible.

MOVING ON AS A BOARD

Once the new executive is on the job, and the executive and the board have identified key challenges and priorities, it's time for the board to return to its traditional governance role. The time after the new executive is hired can be an awkward one for the board. For weeks and even months, the board has been more actively engaged than normal in the day-to-day work of the organization — reviewing finances and operations, ensuring the organization's stability, identifying legacy issues for the new executive to address, and working with the new executive to chart a successful course for the future.

Now, there will be a sense of relief that the search and hiring process is over, but also perhaps a sense of let-down and loss of control as the new executive takes the management reins. The challenge for the board is to extricate itself from operations so the new executive can make a mark on the organization, while at the same time remaining actively engaged in different ways. Job number one for the board is making sure that both the new executive and staff have the resources and the support they need to deliver on the mission of the organization.

A very practical and useful strategy at this stage is getting the board back in touch with best-practice models of governance. This can be especially important if the board has an uneven history of performance, or if the departing executive was an exceptionally good model for board-executive partnership. BoardSource has a number of resources in this area. Consider reviewing *The Ten Basic Responsibilities of Nonprofit Boards* by Richard T. Ingram as a starting point.

CONCLUSION

The board-executive relationship is critically important and complex. Developing this relationship to the level of highly effective teamwork takes time. The steps outlined in this chapter are meant to help jumpstart that process, but ultimately it's going to take attention and work from both the board and the executive. As the case studies on pages 66 and 68 show, the payoff from this investment can be enormous in terms of increasing the mission impact of the organization, not to mention the clarity and resulting job satisfaction for board members and the new executive alike.

MANAGING THE SEARCH AND HIRING PROCESS

At this point in the process, the board has

✓ developed a position profile, compensation plan, and search plan and budget to define the parameters of the search

✓ used advertising, Web postings, and direct contacts to generate a diverse group of qualified candidates for the position

✓ created effective systems for resume management and review, interviews, and reference checks

✓ made an offer to the top finalist for the job and put the matter before the full board for a vote

✓ announced the hiring of the new executive to the organization's audiences through in-person contacts with key stakeholders, phone calls, and other means

✓ created a solid orientation for the new executive and facilitated the executive's introductions to staff, board members, donors, and other audiences

✓ worked with the new executive to develop a leadership agenda for the first 12 to 18 months of the executive's tenure

✓ determined how to monitor and evaluate the new executive's performance over the next 12 to 18 months and beyond

✓ built the foundation for a strong partnership with the new executive to ensure a productive and lasting tenure with the organization

Appendix 1

SAMPLE TRANSITION TIMELINE

Event	Responsible Party	Date
Resignation notice — chief executive gives 90 days' notice		Sept. 1
Board/chief executive discuss departure		Sept. 1–7
Board appoints transition committee	Board Chair	Sept. 7
Transition committee holds organizing meeting	Transition Committee	Sept. 10
Transition committee plans departure announcement	Transition Committee/ PR Consultant	Sept. 10–14
Board chair meets with staff	Board Chair	Sept. 14
Organization announces departure publicly	Board Chair w/ Staff Support	Sept. 15
Transition committee holds planning session w/staff	Transition Committee Chair	Sept. 22
Board holds strategic review and leadership planning meeting	Board	Sept. 27
Transition committee holds meeting to develop job profile and search plan	Transition Committee	Oct. 9
Transition committee launches search	Transition Committee	Oct. 12
Transition committee holds check-in meeting(s)	Transition Committee	TBD
Transition committee holds resume review meeting	Transition Committee	Nov. 28
Transition committee holds round one interviews	Transition Committee	Dec. 8
Transition committee holds second planning session w/staff	Transition Committee Chair	Dec. 10
Semifinalists visit office and meet with staff	Semifinalists	Week of Dec. 10

Event	Responsible Party	Date
Executive committee holds round two interviews	Executive Committee	Dec. 18
Board meets to ratify selection	Board	Dec. 21
Executive gives notice to current employer	–	Dec. 30
Transition committee plans on-boarding process	Transition Committee	Jan. 2
Organization announces new executive	Transition Committee	Feb. 1
New executive starts work	–	March 1
New executive and board embark on orientation/ post-hire process	Various Members of the Executive Committee and Management Staff	Mid- to late March
Chief executive completes 90-day plan	Chief Executive	Early to mid-April
Board chair engages with chief executive in 90-day check-in review	Board Chair Chief Executive	Mid- to late June
Executive committee conducts six-month evaluation of executive	Executive Committee	Mid- to late December
Executive committee conducts annual performance evaluation of executive	Executive Committee	Mid- to late March of the following year

Appendix 2

SAMPLE AGREEMENT AND WORK PLAN FOR INTERIM CHIEF EXECUTIVE

[This sample letter of agreement is sent by the interim chief executive to the board chair.]

[Client]

Dear _____: (Board Chair)

It was a pleasure to speak with you and I am looking forward to working with you as interim chief executive for [organization]. This engagement letter outlines our mutual understanding about the key responsibilities, terms, and fees as well as the agreed-on priorities for the interim period.

POSITION OVERVIEW

The interim chief executive role is to provide management and supervision until a permanent chief executive is hired and to assist the board and staff in preparing the organization for the new executive.

Responsibilities:

Serve as interim chief executive with authority to supervise, on a part-time basis, all staff through the management structure, oversee the day-to-day operations of the organization, and carry out responsibilities determined by the Transition Committee. All hiring and firing of staff, if any, will be done with concurrence of the board chair. [Clarify check-signing authority here: The interim executive is authorized to sign all checks, except checks over $ _____ require a second signature by the treasurer or another officer. OR All checks are to be signed by a board member.] Contracts can be executed only with the written approval of the board.

General Management Duties: [following is just an example]

- Provide supervision of staff, consultants, and coordination and oversight for day-to-day operations.

- Provide leadership in cultivating and managing relations with key stakeholders, members and donors.

- Meet all deadlines from funding or contract sources for applications, reports, and other requirements.

- Assist board in fundraising planning, proposal writing, and event planning as mutually agreed and subject to time availability.

- Provide oversight and review of management systems and recommend changes as needed.

- Support the activities of the board, as agreed, in preparing and recruiting and orienting the new chief executive.

- Carry out other agreed-upon activities based on priorities of the attached work plan.

In addition to providing general management, the preliminary assessment and discussion with the Transition Committee suggest the six priorities outlined in Attachment #1. We will want to establish a communication plan, such as regular conference calls, so that the Transition Committee has adequate access to the interim chief executive for information sharing, strategic discussion, and reporting.

Supervision:

Day-to-day supervision of the interim chief executive is the responsibility of the board chair.

Term, Hours, Fees:

The term of the assignment will be _____ through _____. The termination date is flexible, depending on the progress of the executive search and the organization's needs. The assignment is part time, not to exceed an average of ___ hours per week/___ hours per month.

The interim chief executive will be retained as a consultant, at the rate of $___ per hour. As an independent contractor, the interim chief executive will not be entitled to any employee benefits. Invoices will be submitted monthly and payment is expected within fifteen (15) days. A timesheet will be provided to the board chair or his/her designee for review and approval.

The interim chief executive may terminate this agreement with fifteen (15) days' written notice for any reason, unless a shorter time period is agreed upon. [Organization] may terminate this agreement immediately upon a breach or, if no breach has occurred, upon fifteen (15) days' written notice.

Other Agreements:

[Organization] will provide reimbursement for business-related out-of-pocket expenses, such as approved out-of-the-area travel and local non-commuting travel for [organization] business.

Please indicate your acceptance of this agreement on behalf of [organization] by countersigning below. Thanks again for selecting me as your interim chief executive. I look forward to working with you.

Sincerely,
Jane Q. Interim

ACCEPTED FOR [ORGANIZATION]:

_____   _____

Signature of Board Chair   Date

Sample Agreement (continued)

INTERIM CHIEF EXECUTIVE'S PRIORITIES
NOVEMBER 1, 20XX THROUGH FEBRUARY 28, 20XX

In addition to the general management duties, the following are [organization's] priorities for the interim period:

IMPROVING INTERNAL/EXTERNAL COMMUNICATIONS

-
-
-

UPCOMING ANNUAL EVENT

-
-
-

FUND DEVELOPMENT

-
-
-

STAFF DEVELOPMENT

-
-
-

BOARD RELATIONS/DEVELOPMENT

-
-
-

SYSTEM/PROCEDURES DEVELOPMENT

-
-
-

Appendix 3

CHIEF EXECUTIVE'S POSITION PROFILE AND JOB ANNOUNCEMENT TEMPLATES

NOTE: The position profile is a multipage document that is used to ensure internal agreement about the nature of the job and as a tool to support discussions with serious candidates. The job announcement is one page or less and is used to publicize the job. The announcement might be employed as a paper handout, as an attachment to an e-mail, etc.

POSITION PROFILE: CHIEF EXECUTIVE XYZ NONPROFIT

[*Opening paragraph that sums it all up.*] XYZ Nonprofits is seeking an entrepreneurial chief executive to build on our exceptional eight-year record of....

THE ORGANIZATION

[*Paragraphs about the organization's background.*] XYZ was founded in....

Programs

[*Paragraphs or bullet points about the programs/services.*]

[*Concluding paragraph about the organization's background and key programs or services, budget, staffing and board, and concludes with a link to the Web site.*] XYZ is governed by an XX-member board of directors. The organization's budget is.... Current staffing includes.... More information on XYZ may be found at (Web site).

THE POSITION

[*A paragraph or two about the executive's role and leadership opportunity.*]

[*Bullet points about the 12–18 month priorities.*] Toward these ends, our near-term priorities for the next 12–18 months include (not necessarily in priority order)

- [Bullet points]

Key Responsibilities

[*An opening paragraph followed by several bullet points about the key responsibilities.*] Reporting to the board of directors, the chief executive will provide leadership to the organization and manage its day-to-day affairs...

- [Bullet points]

Experience and Attributes

[*An opening paragraph followed by several bullet points about the experience and attributes.*] Ideal candidates for this position will share our commitment to…and will bring a variety of experiences and attributes to XYZ, including

- [Bullet points]

Salary will be competitive and commensurate with qualifications and experience.

APPLICATION PROCESS

To apply, send an e-mail with a cover letter detailing your qualifications, resume and salary requirements to (e-mail address).

Resumes will be considered until position is filled.

XYZ Nonprofit is an equal opportunity employer.

POSITION ANNOUNCEMENT:
CHIEF EXECUTIVE
XYZ NONPROFIT

[*Opening paragraph that sums it all up.*] XYZ Nonprofits is seeking an entrepreneurial chief executive to build on our exceptional eight-year record of….

[*Paragraph about the organization's background and key programs or services, budget, staffing and board, and concludes with a link to the Web site.*] XYZ was founded in…. XYZ is governed by an XX-member board of directors. The organization's budget is…. Current staffing includes…. More information on XYZ may be found at (Web site).

[*Paragraph about key responsibilities that concludes with a link the full position summary.*] Reporting to the board of directors, the chief executive will provide…. For a full description of the position and its responsibilities, please visit: (Web site).

[*Paragraph identifying the key attribute the organization is seeking followed by a few key bullet points drawn from the attributes section of the position profile. Conclude with education or experience in lieu of education requirement.*] Ideal candidates for this position will share our commitment to…and will bring a variety of experiences and attributes to XYZ, including

- [Bullet point]
- [Bullet point]
- [Bullet point]
- [Bullet point]
- [Bullet point]

- [Bullet point]

- [Education requirement bullet point]

[Conclude with how to apply and EEO statement if applicable. Also include application deadline if one has been established.]

To apply, send an e-mail with a cover letter detailing your qualifications, resume, and salary requirements to (e-mail address).

Resumes will be considered until position is filled. *XYZ nonprofit is an equal opportunity employer.*

Appendix 4

WEB SITES TO POST THE JOB ANNOUNCEMENT AND ADVERTISE THE JOB

NONPROFIT JOB WEB SITES

Best Bets for Executive Jobs (mostly executive and senior-level jobs)

- **www.asaenet.org** (see Career Headquarters) Association with over 25,000 individual members who manage leading trade, professional, and philanthropic associations. Represents 10,000 associations.

- **www.associationjobs.org** (Same Web site as www.CEOUpdate.com)

- **www.CEOUpdate.com** A premier source for up-to-date information on senior-level nonprofit jobs in trade associations, professional societies, cause-oriented organizations, and foundations.

- **www.cof.org** A membership organization of grantmaking foundations and giving programs worldwide. Postings for all levels of philanthropic or related nonprofit positions are welcome.

- **www.ExecSearches.com** Features executive, fundraising, and midlevel job postings in nonprofits, government, health care, and education.

- **www.idealist.org** A portal for anyone interested in nonprofit careers, volunteering, and internships.

- **www.NPTimes.com** The online service of *The Nonprofit Times*.

- **philanthropy.com/jobs/philanthropy careers** is the online job site of *The Chronicle of Philanthropy*.

- **OpportunityNocs.org** Electronic version of a long-established nonprofit job newspaper that started in the San Francisco area.

Other Nonprofit Job Sites (may include executive jobs along with other positions)

- **www.developpro.com** Resources for development professionals, including a jobs board.

- **www.devnetjobs.org** A gateway to international development jobs.

- **www.DeepSweep.com** A free job posting and resume bank for nonprofit employers.

- **www.DotOrgJobs.com** A free online employment resource for nonprofits.

- **www.fdncenter.org/pnd/current/index.html** (Same as Philanthropy News Digest's Job Corner)

- **www.interaction.org/jobs/index.html** Jobs with U.S.-based humanitarian and development organizations with positions available in the United States and overseas.

- **www.internationaljobs.org/hotjobs.html** Mid- and senior-level positions with nonprofit and for-profit organizations, based all around the world, as well as entry-level and internship positions.

- **www.nassembly.org** Jobs at health and human services organizations.

- **www.nonprofitcareer.com** Job and volunteer opportunities.

- **www.nonprofitjobs.org** Fee-based job site for nonprofit organizations.

- **www.NonprofitOyster.com** Fee-based job site for nonprofit organizations.

- **www.pnnonline.org** Fee-based job site for nonprofit organizations.

Regional Sites

- Atlanta: **www.nonprofitgeorgia.org/jobs.html**

- California (Northern): **OpportunityNocs.org** Individual job postings cost $80 for a 30-day listing. www.opportunityknocks.org/index.jsp (Same as OpportunityNocs.org)

- California (Southern): **www.nonprofitdirections.org**

- Washington, D.C.: **www.nonprofitadvancement.org** Center for Nonprofit Advancement Web site.

- Maryland: **www.mdnonprofit.org** (See "Career Bank" link for jobs in Maryland) Members can post jobs for free.

- New England: **www.OpNocsne.org**

- Philadelphia: **www.lasallenonprofitcenter.org/research_pub/joblistings.htm**

- Texas: **www.cnmdallas.org/pages/employ.html**

Print Publications

- *The Chronicle of Philanthropy:* **www.philanthropy.com**

- *The Nonprofit Times:* **www.NPTimes.com**

- Your local daily newspaper

- Print newsletters dedicated to your field/industry

Appendix 5

SAMPLE RESUME SCORING SHEET

Rank each candidate on a scale of 1–3 using the following criteria:

1 = Meets all the criteria. Has all of the required experience, skills, and education. An excellent match for the position, at least on paper.

2 = Meets some the criteria. Has some the required experience, skills, and education. Maybe good or OK match for the position. Might be worth exploring further.

3 = Unqualified. Has little relevant experience or skills.

	Mission Experience	Senior Management Experience	Fundraising Track Record	Staff Supervision Experience	Financial Management Experience	Board Experience	Education	Resume Score
Candidate Name:								
Comments:								
Candidate Name:								
Comments:								
Candidate Name:								
Comments:								
Candidate Name:								
Comments:								
Candidate Name:								
Comments:								
Candidate Name:								
Comments:								
Candidate Name:								
Comments:								
Candidate Name:								
Comments:								
Candidate Name:								
Comments:								
Candidate Name:								
Comments:								

Appendix 6

Sample Vetting Questions/Candidate Questionnaire

1. From your resume, I gather that you are… [currently employed or between positions]?

2. Looking at your current job [or last job if between positions], how did your work (or leadership) enhance the impact of the organization?

   a. Probe for what he/she found when started and what he/she's leaving behind.

3. What are your salary expectations?

4. Have you been responsible for supervising a team of professionals? (Probe for description.)

5. Have you been responsible for preparing and monitoring a budget? (Probe for description.)

6. Have you been directly responsible to a board of directors?

7. Can you give me a quick thumbnail sketch of your work on grants and other fundraising?

8. If I were speaking to your board chair or former supervisor…

   a. What would they say are your strengths?

   b. Your weaknesses?

9. Please describe an experience that you have had (professional or otherwise) where you were involved in developing and implementing a new idea, program, service, or concept.

10. What achievements are your greatest sources of pride?

11. At this point in your personal and professional life, what are the issues/factors that will most influence your next career move?

12. How would you describe the personal values and philosophy that would guide you as you provide leadership in this position?

13. Why do you think you are well suited for the position?

14. If the board were to make you an offer, when would you be available? What notice do you need to give your current employer?

15. Are you under consideration for another position or are you a candidate in another executive search? [If yes] Do you have any active offers or do you anticipate an offer?

16. Any other comments you'd like to make?

17. Is there a question that you would like to pose to us?

Appendix 7

SAMPLE INTERVIEW AGENDA AND QUESTIONS

INTERVIEW AGENDA

- Welcome

- Round-the-table introductions: name, affiliation, and role/involvement with the organization.

- Core questions (below)

- Open questions

- Candidate questions

- Wrap-up

CORE QUESTIONS

1. To get us started, please give us a <u>very brief</u> thumbnail sketch of your career as it leads up to your interest in this position. *Probe:* Why this position at this time?

2. Looking at your last job, what's different about the organization as a direct result of your work there?

3. Please give us an example of a really significant obstacle or challenge that you have faced in your career and how you tackled it.

4. Could you give us an example of a problematic relationship that you turned around... or one that you couldn't turn around and what you learned from that?

5. [This question applies only to membership organizations] How would you begin the process of learning about our members and what they do?

6. What experiences would you draw on to build relationships with our current donors, develop new donors/support, and ensure that our organization meets its fundraising targets?

7. What skills and specific experiences would you draw on to raise the visibility of our organization?

8. As chief executive, what are the key things that you will expect from the board and what should they expect from you?

9. What are some crucial ingredients in fostering high levels of staff performance? *Follow up:* Do you have some examples of putting those into practice?

10. Given what you know about our organization, why do you think you are well suited for the position? What about the job do you think might be most challenging?

ILLEGAL OR INAPPROPRIATE QUESTIONS

Questions pertaining to the following topics should be avoided, as they may be illegal:

- Race, color, or ethnicity

- National origin or birthplace

- Age

- Gender

- Religion

- Political affiliation

- Marital status

- Family issues (number of children, unwed motherhood, family planning, child care needs)

- Sexual orientation

- Arrest record

- Military discharge

- Credit history

- Height and weight

- Disabilities

If in doubt, don't ask.

Appendix 8

Sample Interviewee Rating Criteria

Please check the appropriate rating and add your comments below as desired.

	Outstanding	Strong	Adequate	Weak
Commitment to Mission	☐	☐	☐	☐

Commitment (or ability to commit) to our organization's mission and customers.

Comments:

	Outstanding	Strong	Adequate	Weak
Leadership	☐	☐	☐	☐

Ability to confidently guide the organization — to inspire and enroll people into action.

Comments:

	Outstanding	Strong	Adequate	Weak
Entrepreneurship	☐	☐	☐	☐

Ability to understand our organization's primary customer and develop a vision, strategies, and strategic direction that serve the customers and deliver our organization's mission.

Comments:

	Outstanding	Strong	Adequate	Weak
Fundraising	☐	☐	☐	☐

Ability to provide leadership to (and involvement in) the fundraising efforts that are important to our organization.

Comments:

	Outstanding	Strong	Adequate	Weak
General Management & Internal Operations/Systems	☐	☐	☐	☐

Ability to guide development of overall structure, methods, and controls — organize the whole, plan the action/follow the plan, develop the methods/systems, and exercise control.

Comments:

	Outstanding	Strong	Adequate	Weak
Staff Leadership/Supervision	☐	☐	☐	☐

Ability to select and develop staff and motivate the best work from them. Has a commitment to staff development.

Comments:

	Outstanding	Strong	Adequate	Weak
Financial Leadership	☐	☐	☐	☐

Ability to provide the appropriate level of guidance, oversight, and involvement in our organization's financial management and its development. Is financially literate.

Comments:

	Outstanding	Strong	Adequate	Weak
External Visibility & Communications	☐	☐	☐	☐

Ability to communicate clearly with appropriate audiences using appropriate means. Ability to build the organization's stature and raise its profile.

Comments:

	Outstanding	Strong	Adequate	Weak
Board Relations/Development	☐	☐	☐	☐

Ability to be an effective leadership partner with the board and to support the board's work and its development.

Comments:

	Outstanding	Strong	Adequate	Weak
Cultural Competency	☐	☐	☐	☐

Ability to relate to people of varied economic, racial, ethnic, and religious backgrounds.

Comments:

Appendix 9

REFERENCE CHECKING TOOLS

E-MAIL TO SECURE REFERENCES

Dear [Name],

Regarding your application for the XYZ Nonprofit Chief Executive position, we need to contact your personal references. Toward that end, we request at least five references with at least one in each of the following categories:

- Someone who has supervised you (at least two of these, please)

- Someone you have supervised

- A peer or colleague who is familiar with your professional work

Please e-mail them to me as soon as possible.

Regards,

[Name and e-mail]

Transition Committee Chair

QUESTIONS TO ASK REFERENCES

1. May I ask in what capacity you have known [candidate] and how long have you known him/her?

2. How would you describe his/her major strengths?

3. Do you have perspective on his/her leadership skills? How did the organization change under his/her leadership? What are some of the challenges and opportunities he/she may have faced and how did he/she address them?

4. Have you had an opportunity to observe [candidate's] communications skills? Are there communication situations or approaches where you think he/she excels?

   a. How about his/her ability to communicate with diverse constituencies?

5. Do you have any perspective on [candidate's] financial management abilities?

   a. [If yes] How would your rate his/her financial management abilities: Strong, so-so, or weak?

   b. [Probe for comments.]

6. Do you have any perspective on [candidate's] fundraising abilities?

  a. [If yes] How would your rate his/her fundraising abilities: Strong, so-so, or weak?

  b. [Probe for comments.]

7. Do you have any perspective on [candidate's] skill at selecting and managing a staff, and building a team?

  a. [If yes] How would your rate his/her abilities in this area: Strong, so-so, or weak?

  b. [Probe for comments.]

8. Do you have any perspective on [candidate's] skill at marketing an organization or building public awareness?

  a. [If yes] How would your rate his/her abilities: Strong, so-so, or weak?

  b. [Probe for comments.]

9. Managing a small nonprofit involves managing a lot of competing demands. Have you had occasion to observe [candidate's] work ethic, approach to time management, and his/her sense of organization and planning? How would you describe?

10. One of the major aspects of the job is working with a board. [Describe board situation, dynamics.] Do you have any comments on how [candidate] might excel?

  a. What aspects of this do you think he/she would find most challenging?

11. Given the thumbnail sketch of the job that I provided at the start of the interview…

  a. Are there particular aspects of the job at which you think [candidate] will excel? [Probe]

  b. Are there aspects of the job that you think he/she would be better off leaving to others? [Probe]

12. Is there anything else you think it would be helpful for the committee to know as we go forward in this process?

Appendix 10

Sample Employment Offer Letter

[Date]

[Name & Address]

Dear [Candidate Name]:

The Board of Directors of [organization] is pleased to extend to you an offer of employment as its Chief Executive. The following outlines the specifics of the offer:

1. Starting Salary: [Salary expressed in monthly terms. Stating an annual figure could be construed as an annual contract.]

2. Benefits Package: [May just refer to employee handbook or personnel policies. If no handbook or policy is available, or if the benefits are to be different, then specify here.]

   a. Health Insurance: ...

   b. Retirement: ...

   c. Annual Leave: ...

   d. Holidays: [Holidays should be the same as for other employees]

3. Relocation Stipend: [If applicable]

4. Performance Goals: The board (or chair) will meet with you within the first six weeks of your employment to begin setting performance goals and the protocol for evaluating your performance. In large part, this will be based on a "leadership agenda" that outlines key priorities, which we expect you to develop for our review, discussion, and approval. You and the board will evaluate your performance after your first six months of employment against these mutually agreed goals.

5. [Use this only if an at-will state.] Although the board expects that the relationship with you will be long-term and mutually rewarding, you are an at-will employee. You and the board have the right to terminate employment at any time for any reason [add notice period here if there is one, e.g., "with 30 days' notice"].

6. Full-time employment as chief executive is to begin on [date].

On behalf of the Board of Directors, I am excited and delighted to extend the offer and look forward to a successful professional relationship.

Sincerely,
[Signature of Board Chair/Transition Committee Chair]

Acknowledged:

_____   _____

Candidate's Name   Date

Appendix 11

SAMPLE REGRETS LETTERS

SAMPLE REGRETS E-MAIL (OR LETTER) FOR CANDIDATES WHO WERE NOT INTERVIEWED

Dear [Name]:

On behalf of XYZ Nonprofit, I want to thank you for your interest in the chief executive position. I am writing to inform you that the search for this position has concluded with the selection of a new executive.

The transition committee was faced with the challenge of choosing among many qualified candidates for the open position. We certainly appreciate your taking the time to share your credentials with us and wish you all the best in your professional pursuits and goals.

Sincerely,
[Name]

Transition Committee Chair

SAMPLE REGRETS LETTER FOR CANDIDATES WHO WERE INTERVIEWED

Dear [Name]:

On behalf of the board of directors of XYZ Nonprofit, I want to thank you for your interest in the chief executive position and for taking the time to interview with us. I am writing to inform you that the search has concluded with the selection of a new executive.

The transition committee was faced with the challenge of choosing among many qualified candidates for the open position. We certainly appreciate your taking the time to share your credentials with us and wish you all the best in your professional pursuits and goals.

While in the end we hired another candidate, we want you to know that we were impressed with your qualifications and abilities. In the process of interviewing you, I am sure that we gained fresh insights on our work and the challenges we face.

Thank you and best wishes in all your professional pursuits and goals.

Sincerely,
[Name]

Transition Committee Chair

Appendix 12

SAMPLE CHIEF EXECUTIVE 90-DAY ENTRY PLAN

(Assumes that the start date is Jan. 1)

BUILDING RELATIONSHIPS

- Staff

  - Meet with each staff member (individually or in teams) within my first two weeks.

    · Assess their perspectives and evaluation of our organization

    · Impart my management, mission philosophy, and key expectations.

    · Hold first monthly all-staff meeting by March 31.

- Board Members

  - Hold face-to-face or phone conversations with each member of the board within first 30 days.

    · Ask about specific expectations for my first 12 to 18 months.

    · Inquire about concerns.

    · Discuss their sense of the vision for our organization's future.

- Key Donors

  - Plan joint visits with former CEO by February 15. (if agreed)

  - Complete joint visits with donors by March 31.

  - Initiate individual conversations with at least three donors per week until development director position filled, then 6 to 8 per week.

  - Recruit table captains and sponsors for the benefit breakfast by March 31.

- Other Close-In Stakeholders (collaboration partners, etc.)

  - Visit each program sponsor by March 31.

  - Introduce self to leaders of our collaboration partners by March 31.

- Other Community Stakeholders (powers-that-be in the community)

  - Introduce self to relevant senior-level county and city staff by March 15.

  - Meet with county board chair and all commissioners covering our service area by March 31.

Developing an Understanding and Assuming Appropriate Responsibility for the Organization's Operations

- Programs

  - Receive briefings from key staff regarding the programs they direct by February 1.

  - Review key grant agreements by February 1.

  - Meet with all significant grantors by March 31.

- Finances

  - Review current financial statements (profit and loss, balance sheet, and cash flow projections) by February 1. Review at least monthly thereafter.

  - Meet in person with accountant and treasurer at least once each month.

  - Meet with the finance committee by February 15 and at least monthly thereafter.

  - Ensure signatories on all accounts are up to date by February 1.

  - Provide updated budgetary information to key staff on a weekly basis by March 1.

  - Provide strategy to finance committee to address equipment upgrades by the committee's March meeting.

- Fundraising (see "Donors" under "Building Relationships")

  - Assess skill requirements and develop plan for filling vacant development director position by February 15; hire a development director by March 15.

  - Assess overall development resources by February 28.

  - Develop plan to address donor acknowledgment issues by March 1.

- Marketing

  - Develop media plan to include news articles and coverage of major events by February 15.

  - Review current marketing materials by March 15.

  - Develop process for evaluating possible changes in Web site by April 1.

- Support for Board of Directors

  - Maintain personal contact with all board members at least once per month.

  - Return all messages and phone calls within 24 hours.

  - Consult with the executive committee on agenda for March board meeting.

  - Distribute a monthly chief executive update to the board beginning on March 1.

BUILDING THE ORGANIZATION'S CAPACITY

- Take the initiative and develop a plan to lead the board to formulate and implement its vision regarding

    - Relocation and expansion of office

    - The shape of the "next leap" in services, e.g., expanding our meals program, etc.

    - Broadening the base of major donors

    - Implementing a planned giving initiative

PERSONAL LEARNING GOALS AND SUPPORT NEEDS

- Participate in a new executive program

- Seek professional training in board relations, especially regarding building donor support and the tension between governance and management.

- Identify and hire an executive coach.

- Participate in an executive peer support program

Appendix 13

BOARDSOURCE EXECUTIVE SEARCH — NEEDS ASSESSMENT

This survey is designed to help those involved in the search for a new chief executive by gathering information from key constituents. This is only one step in the process of your search for a new executive but should provide useful information on the current capacity of the organization and the board, as well as the future needs of the organization. The assessment can also provide a snapshot of the strengths and weaknesses of the outgoing chief executive and how this shapes the search for the incoming chief executive.

Each organization should determine which individuals should be invited to take the survey. Each group of individuals, including board members, staff, and donors, will bring a unique but valuable perspective on how to shape the search for a new executive. Typically an in-depth interview would be used to get the perspective of the outgoing chief executive, but the questions in this survey can serve as a guide about which areas to cover.

Staff — in most instances only key or senior staff would be asked for input.

Donors — this depends on the type of relationship and involvement with key donors.

To score the answers: Answers for each question have been assigned a numerical value. All answers for a single question should be counted and averaged. You may wish to do a more detailed analysis and break scores out by groups, i.e., separate staff scores from the board's scores.

If you are interested in using BoardSource to administer the survey, please contact eproducts@boardsource.org or 800-883-6262 for more information and an estimate of cost.

BoardSource kindly acknowledges and thanks Sally Sterling, Spencer Stuart, Mary Tydings, Russell Reynolds Associates, and Deborah S. Hechinger, former President and CEO of BoardSource, for collaborating on the development of the Executive Search — Needs Assessment.

STEP 1: DISTRIBUTE THE SURVEY AND COLLECT RESPONSES

Distribute the questionnaire to all individuals either by U. S. mail or e-mail. A firm deadline for completion and return of the questionnaire should accompany its distribution. The typical time frame is about 10-15 days. A letter from the board chair or person heading up the search process, defining the process and explaining how the information will be used along with the importance of individual participation in the survey helps generate enthusiasm for the process. The search committee needs to decide whether to ask people to add their names to the survey or whether answers should be submitted confidentially.

STEP 2: ANALYZE THE SURVEY DATA

When all surveys are returned, the comments and responses need to be compiled into a survey report. The compilation and analysis of the responses to the survey can be completed by the board chair, the search committee or an outside consultant.

If you choose to score the results yourself please follow these steps.

a. Gather all surveys that were returned and count the number of answer in each box, i.e., for question #1, 2 people selected "Strongly Disagree"; 3 selected "2"; 3 selected "Strongly Agree."

b. Multiply the number of answers by the numerical value assigned to each answer which is shown in the top row in each section.

c. To calculate the average, add the scores and divide the sum by the number of people who answered the question.

	Strongly Disagree		Agree		Strongly Agree	
	1	2	3	4	5	
Mission, Strategy, Programs						
1. The current mission statement is appropriate over the next 2-4 years?	☐	☐	☐	☐	☐	
a. Count the number of answers in each box	2	3	8	5	3	21
b. Multiply the number of answers by the numerical value assigned to each answer	2 x 1 = 2	3 x 2 = 6	8 x 3 = 24	5 x 4 = 20	3 x 5 = 15	Total = 67
c. Add the scores and divide the sum by the number of people who answered the question.	67/21 = 3.42					Average = 3.19
2. The organization has been effective in meeting its current mission and objectives.	0	2	6	12	1	21
(a) count; (b) multiply; (c) average	0 x 1 = 0	2x2 = 4	6 x 3 = 18	12 x 4 = 48	1 x 5 = 5	75/21= 3.57

Step 3: Compile the Survey Report

Once you have completed the calculations for each question you will need to transfer the information into a report that can be distributed and shared with the search committee and other appropriate individuals. When completing the report, it is important to show how many individuals selected each answer for a question as well as the average score for each question.

We suggest using this format for the survey report:

	Strongly Disagree		Agree		Strongly Agree	Average Score
	1	2	3	4	5	
Mission, Strategy, Programs						
1. The current mission statement is appropriate over the next 2-4 years?	2	3	8	5	3	3.19
2. The organization has been effective in meeting its current mission and objectives.	0	2	6	12	1	3.57
3. The organization needs to change its programs and services.	2	1	12	5	1	3.10

BOARDSOURCE EXECUTIVE SEARCH — NEEDS ASSESSMENT

SECTION A: ORGANIZATION PROFILE

1. Is the organization looking to

   ☐ Scale back or downsize

   ☐ Maintain with improvements

   ☐ Grow or modify programs

2. Describe the culture of the organization.

3. What is your role within this organization?

   ☐ Staff

   ☐ Board member

   ☐ Donor

   ☐ Consultant

   ☐ Other — please specify:

SECTION B: CHALLENGES AND OPPORTUNITIES

Please indicate how strongly you disagree or agree with the following statements.

	Strongly Disagree 1	2	Agree 3	4	Strongly Agree 5
Mission, Strategy, Programs					
1. The current mission statement is appropriate over the next 2–4 years.	☐	☐	☐	☐	☐
2. The organization has been effective in meeting its current mission and objectives.	☐	☐	☐	☐	☐
3. The organization needs to change its programs and services.	☐	☐	☐	☐	☐

	Strongly Disagree 1	2	Agree 3	4	Strongly Agree 5

Marketing and Positioning

4. The organization has an effective communications and marketing strategy. ☐ ☐ ☐ ☐ ☐

5. The organization has a positive image in the community. ☐ ☐ ☐ ☐ ☐

6. The organization has established mutually beneficial collaborations and partnerships. ☐ ☐ ☐ ☐ ☐

Fundraising

Skip questions 7–9 if your organization does not receive charitable contributions.

7. The organization effectively raises funds to accomplish its mission and goals. ☐ ☐ ☐ ☐ ☐

8. The organization maintains good relationships with its major donors. ☐ ☐ ☐ ☐ ☐

9. The organization needs to undertake a major fundraising campaign in the next 1–2 years. ☐ ☐ ☐ ☐ ☐

Finance and Administration

10. The organization is financially sound. ☐ ☐ ☐ ☐ ☐

11. The organization is stronger now than it was three years ago. ☐ ☐ ☐ ☐ ☐

12. The organization uses technology to further its mission and to streamline its operations. ☐ ☐ ☐ ☐ ☐

13. The current organizational structure can sustain the organization for the next 1–2 years. ☐ ☐ ☐ ☐ ☐

14. Describe the major threats or challenges facing the organization in the next three years.

SECTION C: ORGANIZATIONAL CAPACITY

Rate the organization's strength in these areas:

	Weak 1	2	Adequate 3	4	Strong 5
1. Development and delivery of programs	☐	☐	☐	☐	☐
2. Education and outreach	☐	☐	☐	☐	☐
3. Marketing and communications	☐	☐	☐	☐	☐
4. Fundraising and resource development	☐	☐	☐	☐	☐
5. Lobbying/advocacy	☐	☐	☐	☐	☐
6. Human resources and management structure	☐	☐	☐	☐	☐
7. Administration and operations (finance, technology, etc.)	☐	☐	☐	☐	☐

Indicate how strongly you disagree or agree with the following staff issues:

	Strongly Disagree 1	2	Agree 3	4	Strongly Agree 5
8. Prior to announcing the chief executive's departure, staff morale was high.	☐	☐	☐	☐	☐
9. The staff works well together.	☐	☐	☐	☐	☐
10. Senior staff works well with the board.	☐	☐	☐	☐	☐
11. Staff members have sufficient resources to do their jobs well.	☐	☐	☐	☐	☐
12. Staff anticipates a difficult transition.	☐	☐	☐	☐	☐
13. There is likely to be staff turnover due to the executive transition.	☐	☐	☐	☐	☐
14. Significant staff turnover during the transition would put the organization at risk.	☐	☐	☐	☐	☐
15. What will most challenge staff during the transition?					

SECTION D: BOARD PERFORMANCE

Indicate how strongly you disagree or agree with the following statements.

		Strongly Disagree 1	2	Agree 3	4	Strongly Agree 5
1.	The board is engaged in setting the organization's strategic direction and priorities.	☐	☐	☐	☐	☐
2.	The board monitors financial performance on a regular basis.	☐	☐	☐	☐	☐
3.	The board participates in fundraising activities.	☐	☐	☐	☐	☐
4.	The board opens doors within the community for the organization.	☐	☐	☐	☐	☐
5.	Most board members are actively engaged in the work of the board.	☐	☐	☐	☐	☐
6.	A climate of mutual trust and respect exists between the outgoing chief executive and board.	☐	☐	☐	☐	☐
7.	A climate of mutual trust and respect exists among board members.	☐	☐	☐	☐	☐
8.	The respective roles of the board and staff are clearly defined and understood.	☐	☐	☐	☐	☐
9.	The board assesses the chief executive's performance in a systematic and fair way.	☐	☐	☐	☐	☐
10.	The process for determining the chief executive's compensation is objective and adequate.	☐	☐	☐	☐	☐

SECTION E: THE NEW CHIEF EXECUTIVE

Describe the level of abilities of the outgoing chief executive.

		Weak 1	2	Adequate 3	4	Strong 5
1.	Effective spokesperson for the organization	☐	☐	☐	☐	☐
2.	Knowledgeable about programs and services	☐	☐	☐	☐	☐
3.	Knowledgeable about financial management	☐	☐	☐	☐	☐
4.	Successful fundraiser	☐	☐	☐	☐	☐
5.	Created productive partnerships	☐	☐	☐	☐	☐
6.	Worked effectively with staff	☐	☐	☐	☐	☐
7.	Worked effectively with board	☐	☐	☐	☐	☐

Indicate how important the following experiences are for the incoming chief executive.

		Not Important 1	2	Important 3	4	Essential 5
8.	Experienced chief executive	☐	☐	☐	☐	☐
9.	5+ years experience as senior executive	☐	☐	☐	☐	☐
10.	Recognized leader within the industry	☐	☐	☐	☐	☐
11.	Experience in corporate world	☐	☐	☐	☐	☐
12.	Experience in public sector	☐	☐	☐	☐	☐
13.	Experience in nonprofit sector	☐	☐	☐	☐	☐
14.	International experience	☐	☐	☐	☐	☐
15.	Commitment to stay 5+ years	☐	☐	☐	☐	☐

16. What will be the biggest challenge for the new chief executive?

Indicate how important the following skills and abilities are for the incoming chief executive.
Please select no more than three abilities as essential.

	Not Important 1	2	Important 3	4	Essential 5
17. Ability to strengthen programs	☐	☐	☐	☐	☐
18. Ability to manage complex operation	☐	☐	☐	☐	☐
19. Ability to manage and lead change	☐	☐	☐	☐	☐
20. Ability to raise funds	☐	☐	☐	☐	☐
21. Ability to increase earned revenue	☐	☐	☐	☐	☐
22. Ability to lobby and advocate	☐	☐	☐	☐	☐
23. Ability to develop a high profile with key outside constituents	☐	☐	☐	☐	☐

	Not Important 1	2	Important 3	4	Essential 5
24. Ability to network and build partnerships	☐	☐	☐	☐	☐
25. Ability to build an effective working relationship with the board	☐	☐	☐	☐	☐
26. Ability to build a strong senior staff team	☐	☐	☐	☐	☐

27. Describe the ideal candidate.

Appendix 14

About the CD-ROM

The attached CD-ROM contains electronic forms of the preceding appendices. The forms on this CD-ROM are published by BoardSource and can be used as-is or, in some cases, customized for your organization's needs.

The files on this CD-ROM are in three formats:

- Microsoft® Word for Windows and Macintosh, version 6.0 (.doc)

- Adobe® Reader files (.pdf)

- Generic text files (.txt)

The documents for each format are contained in the appropriately-named subdirectory.

The CD-ROM is the copyright of BoardSource and is protected under federal copyright law. Any unlawful duplication of this CD-ROM is in violation of that copyright. Before customizing Microsoft® Word or text documents, save a backup copy on your hard drive, and work from the copy on your hard drive.

Contents

Microsoft® Word files

- Sample Transition Timeline

- Sample Agreement and Work Plan for Interim Chief Executive

- Chief Executive's Position Profile and Job Announcement Templates

- Web Sites to Post the Job Announcement and Advertise the Job

- Sample Resume Scoring Sheet

- Sample Vetting Questions/Candidate Questionnaire

- Reference Checking Tools

- Sample Interview Agenda and Questions

- Sample Interviewee Rating Criteria

- Sample Employment Offer Letter

- Sample Regrets Letter

- Sample Chief Executive 90-Day Entry Plan

- BoardSource Executive Search — Needs Assessment

Adobe® files

- Sample Transition Timeline

- Sample Agreement and Work Plan for Interim Chief Executive

- Chief Executive's Position Profile and Job Announcement Templates

- Web Sites to Post the Job Announcement and Advertise the Job

- Sample Resume Scoring Sheet

- Sample Vetting Questions/Candidate Questionnaire

- Reference Checking Tools

- Sample Interview Agenda and Questions

- Sample Interviewee Rating Criteria

- Sample Employment Offer Letter

- Sample Regrets Letter

- Sample Chief Executive 90-Day Entry Plan

- BoardSource Executive Search — Needs Assessment

Generic text files

- Sample Transition Timeline

- Sample Agreement and Work Plan for Interim Chief Executive

- Chief Executive's Position Profile and Job Announcement Templates

- Web Sites to Post the Job Announcement and Advertise the Job

- Sample Resume Scoring Sheet

- Sample Vetting Questions/Candidate Questionnaire

- Reference Checking Tools

- Sample Interview Agenda and Questions

- Sample Interviewee Rating Criteria

- Sample Employment Offer Letter

- Sample Regrets Letter

- Sample Chief Executive 90-Day Entry Plan

- BoardSource Executive Search — Needs Assessment

We hope you enjoy the flexibility and customization capabilities of electronic text. If you have any questions regarding the files on this CD-ROM, call BoardSource at 800-883-6262.

BoardSource
Suite 900
1828 L Street, NW
Washington, DC 20036-5104
202-452-6262
Fax 202-452-6299

Suggested Resources

Adams, Tom. *Capturing the Power of Leadership Change: Using Executive Transition Management to Strengthen Organizational Capacity*. Executive Transition Monograph Series, Volume 1. Baltimore, MD: Annie E. Casey Foundation, 2004. (Available at www.aecf.org/KnowledgeCenter/PublicationsSeries/ExecutiveTransitionMonographs.aspx) This report highlights the challenges associated with executive transitions and introduces the executive management transition model. It also details opportunities for funders to further develop and implement strategies to better cope with executive management transitions.

Adams, Tom. *Founder Transitions: Creating Good Endings and New Beginnings*. Executive Transition Monograph Series, Volume 3. Baltimore, MD: Annie E. Casey Foundation, 2005. (Available at www.aecf.org/KnowledgeCenter/PublicationsSeries/ ExecutiveTransitionMonographs.aspx.) This guide examines the unique challenges presented by transitions involving founders or long-term executives. It provides clear advice for executives and their boards in confronting the complex issues these transitions present.

Adams, Tom. Stepping Up, Staying Engaged: Succession Planning and Executive Transition Management for Nonprofit Boards of Directors. Executive Transition Monograph Series, Volume 5. Baltimore, MD: Annie E. Casey Foundation, 2006 (Available at www.aecf.org/KnowledgeCenter/PublicationsSeries/ ExecutiveTransitionMonographs.aspx.) This publication provides a set of practical perspectives, hands-on tools, brief case studies, and useful resources to help board chairs, officers, and members take a proactive approach to preparing their organizations for a transition.

Axelrod, Nancy R. *Chief Executive Succession Planning: The Board's Role in Securing Your Organization's Future*.Washington, DC: BoardSource, 2002. How ready are you for a leadership transition? In *Chief Executive Succession Planning*, author Nancy R. Axelrod explains why it is important for your board to have a leadership transition plan whether or not you anticipate an upcoming executive search. Learn how to devise an ongoing chief executive officer succession plan that is linked to the strategic planning, mission, and vision of your organization. Help your board prepare for the future by tying the needs of the organization into the chief executive officer job description and chief executive officer evaluation.

Bell, Jeanne, Richard Moyers, and Timothy Wolfred. *Daring to Lead 2006*. CompassPoint and Eugene and Agnes E. Meyer Foundation, 2006. (Available at www.compasspoint.org/assets/194_daringtolead06final.pdf.) *Daring to Lead 2006* is a comprehensive national study of executive leadership at community-based nonprofits. Based on nearly 2,000 surveys from eight metropolitan areas, the report provides current data on executive turnover, compensation, career plans, and retirement. It also explores leading causes of executive burnout — in particular, widespread frustration with boards of directors and funders. It identifies the skills that community-based executives most want and need to build along with the professional development strategies that they employ. The report concludes with recommendations to executives, boards, funders, and capacity builders.

Connolly, Paul M. *Navigating the Organizational Lifecycle: A Capacity-Building Guide for Nonprofit Leaders*. Washington, DC: BoardSource, 2006. Understand, prepare for, and navigate the lifecycle passages and changes experienced by nonprofits. Learn how to assess a nonprofit organization's stage of development in order to align capacities, manage organizational transitions, and anticipate future challenges. One of the key phases during an organization's lifecycle is the hiring of the first chief executive.

Cornelius, Marla, Patrick Corvington and Albert Ruesga. *Ready to Lead? Next Generation Leaders Speak Out*. Jointly published by CompassPoint Nonprofit Services, The Annie E. Casey Foundation, The Meyer Foundation, and Idealist.org, 2008. (Available at www.meyerfoundation.org/downloads/ready_to_lead/ReadytoLead2008.pdf.) A skilled, committed, and diverse pool of next generation leaders would like to be nonprofit executives in the future, but concerns about insufficient work-life balance and lack of earning potential may keep them from it. This national survey of 6,000 emerging nonprofit leaders, produced by the Meyer Foundation in partnership with the Annie E. Casey Foundation and others, presents challenges and recommendations for training and supporting future nonprofit executives.

Gilvar, Barbara J. *The Art of Hiring Leaders: A Guide for Nonprofit Organizations*. Boston, MA: Gilvar Publications, 2007. Each executive search or executive transition is critical for an organization's future and this book, based on the author's more than 25 years' experience as an executive search and transition consultant, is a thorough guide for nonprofit leadership searches. *The Art of Hiring Leaders* explains the executive search process or executive transition so that search committees and boards can complete successful executive search processes.

Kunreuther, Frances. *Up Next: Generation Change and Leadership of Nonprofit Organizations*. Executive Transition Monograph Series, Volume 6. Baltimore, MD: Annie E. Casey Foundation, 2008. (Available at www.aecf.org/KnowledgeCenter/ PublicationsSeries/ExecutiveTransitionMonographs.aspx). Research indicates that leadership transitions from the Baby Boom generation to Generations X and Y will become more common within the nonprofit sector. This report delivers a series of recommendations on how a variety of stakeholders can improve the hand-off from this generation of leaders to the next.

Linnell, Deborah. "Boards and Leadership Hires: How to Get It Right." *Nonprofit Quarterly*, Spring 2008. How a board handles leadership transitions can have powerful and long-lasting effects. In this article, Deborah Linnell takes on the reasons why boards may approach the process largely unprepared and she examines common mistakes and provides practical advice on how to avoid them. A must-read for boards no matter how close or far from a transition.

Mayer, Daniel Y. *Filling the Gap: The Interim Executive Director Solution*. Chicago, IL: Illinois Arts Alliance Foundation, 2005. Taking a page from other fields that have learned the benefits of interim leadership, author Daniel Y. Mayer uses his own experience as an interim executive director (IED) to walk the reader through the issues and questions related to using IEDs to manage leadership transition. This guidebook will prove helpful to staff and board members of arts organizations in need of an IED as well as consultants and other individuals who are considering becoming an IED. Includes an IED job description and "first day on the job" to-do list, a discussion on the role of the artistic director in the transition process, and an organizational diagnostic list, as well as sample employment contracts and a detailed resource list for further reading.

Mintz, Joshua, and Jane Pierson. *Assessment of the Chief Executive*. Washington, DC: BoardSource, 2005. This flexible and practical tool is designed to assist boards in their annual responsibility for assessing the performance of the chief executive. After discussing the benefits of assessment, the user's guide suggests a process and provides a questionnaire that addresses every major area of responsibility. Also included is a self-evaluation form for the executive to complete and share with the board. This resource is also available in a quick and easy-to-use online version.

Neighborhood Reinvestment Corporation. *Managing Executive Transitions*. Neighborhood Reinvestment Corporation, 1999. (Available at www.nw.org/network/ pubs/studies/documents/executiveTransitionsHandbook.pdf.) The importance of an effective, efficient, and dynamic chief executive to the success of the nonprofit organization cannot be overstated. Whatever the circumstances, the process of executive transition is much the same and the guidelines in this book can be applied universally. This handbook addresses three phases of executive transitions: Getting Ready, Recruiting and Hiring, and Post-Hiring.

Weisman, Carol, and Richard I. Goldbaum. *Losing Your Executive Director Without Losing Your Way: The Nonprofit's Guide to Executive Turnover*. San Francisco, CA: Jossey-Bass, 2004. *Losing Your Executive Director Without Losing Your Way* is a practical guide for board members and executives who must guide their nonprofits through the difficult transition of replacing the key member of their organization and shows how to make this transition a positive event. The authors explain how boards can bridge the gap between executive directors and learn to use the transition period as a strategic opportunity. Using this resource, board chairs and members will learn what they need to know to recruit and train the new executive director and help the new chief executive take charge of the organization.

Wolfred, Tim. *Building Leaderful Organizations: Succession Planning for Nonprofits*. Executive Transition Monograph Series, Volume 6. Baltimore, MD: Annie E. Casey Foundation, 2008. (Available at www.aecf.org/KnowledgeCenter/PublicationsSeries/ ExecutiveTransitionMonographs.aspx.) The development of leadership skills throughout an organization is a key strategy for succession planning and strengthening capacity. This publication presents emergency succession planning tools (an important "risk management" practice). It offers executive directors concrete guidance for thinking about when and how to leave an organization. It also includes suggestions for boards in being proactive in assuring the sustainability of the organizations for which they are responsible.

Wolfred, Tim. *Interim Executive Directors: The Power in the Middle*. Executive Transition Monograph Series, Volume 2. San Francisco: The Evelyn and Walter Hass, Jr., 2005. (Available at www.aecf.org/KnowledgeCenter/PublicationsSeries /ExecutiveTransitionMonographs.aspx.) This paper explores the benefits and basics of using an interim executive director during a leadership transition. It also highlights some considerations that organizations should take into account when deciding whether or not to use an interim executive director.

Wolfred, Tim. "Stepping Up: A Board's Challenger on Leadership Transition." *Nonprofit Quarterly*, Winter 2002. (Available at www.compasspoint.org/assets /225_steppingupaboardschalleng.pdf.) Tim Wolfred guides the board with handling executive transition through pleasure and pain. Several case studies elaborate the various challenges the board and the organization have to face during the hiring and transition process.

www.transtionguides.com is an online resource providing background and tools on nonprofit executive transition management and leadership succession.

About the Author

Don Tebbe is Managing Partner of TransitionGuides, a Washington, D.C.-based consulting company that pioneered executive transition management for nonprofits, and enables organizations to capitalize on opportunities that come with transitions. Don leads executive transition and search projects and serves as the practice leader for TransitionGuides' leadership transition services. Don has been leading executive search and transition projects since 1995. He spent his first decade in the nonprofit sector as an executive for several statewide organizations and as a founder and leader in several national groups. He was a cofounder of the National Council of Nonprofit Associations, served as one of the early leaders in the movement to develop statewide associations of nonprofits, and helped form a national unemployment insurance trust. Since starting his consulting practice in 1993, he has focused on advising nonprofits on leadership transitions, as well as helping them develop more effective strategies and business models. He has served a wide variety of organizations from grassroots startups to international organizations, including the world's largest child welfare organization. Don is the author of *For the Good of the Cause: Board Building Lessons from Highly Effective Nonprofits*, a report based on case studies that explored the link between governing board behavior and nonprofit effectiveness.

Don holds a BA in history from the University of Illinois–Springfield where he has also pursued graduate studies in nonprofit administration. He can be reached at TransitionGuides, 1751 Elton Road, Suite 204, Silver Spring MD 20903. Phone: (301) 439-6635, E-mail: dtebbe@transitionguides.com.

AUTHOR ACKNOWLEDGEMENTS

The ideas in this book are the product of a 23-year journey. While it is impossible to thank everyone along the way, I owe substantial debt of gratitude to the following:

- Tom Adams, my business partner and president of TransitionGuides, for his pioneering leadership over the past 15 years that has helped put Executive Transition Management and succession planning on the radar screen for many nonprofits.

- Tim Wolfred, Director of Leadership Services, CompassPoint Nonprofit Services, who's been a very generous colleague and collaborator, and a leader in generating a new understanding about nonprofit leadership

- The staff and leadership of the Annie E. Casey Foundation for their sponsorship of a learning community of executive transition practitioners and their financial support that makes executive transition management available to their grantees

- Bob Kardon, former executive director of the Center for Excellence in Nonprofits and The California Association of Nonprofits, who's been my mentor and thinking partner on all matters nonprofit for the past 20 years

- Our dedicated team at TransitionGuides — a group of extraordinary consultants and professionals dedicated to creating a world that is just, caring, and sustainable